An African Odyssey

An African Odyssey
Evolution, posture and the
work of F.M. Alexander

A Memoir
by Hugh Massey

With a Foreword
by Walter Carrington

Pomegranate
Books

First published in 2001 by Pomegranate Books

Printed in Great Britain by Antony Rowe Ltd, Chippenham, Wilts

ISBN 1-84289-000-X

Pomegranate Books
3 Brynland Avenue, Bristol BS7 9DR, England
www.pomegranatebooks.co.uk

CONTENTS

Illustrations

Before page 9
Map of French Cameroons (1920)
Before page 17
The Author
Before page 99
Hugh Massey with his wife and daughter
Hugh Massey in Morocco

French Cameroons
from *Philips New Handy General
Atlas and Gazetteer* (1920)

The Author

FOREWORD

This is an amazing story told by an extraordinary man. For most of Word War II Hugh Massey was living in one of the wildest parts of Africa - the French Cameroon, amongst the pigmies and the chimpanzees. But, after his hazardous return journey to England, he developed severe pulmonary tuberculosis and began his long struggle against the disease. At that time no effective medical remedy had been discovered and the outcome was usually fatal. In his case, however, the story was very different.

Since I was closely involved with this part of his narrative, I can vouch for many of the remarkable details. I can also supply some explanations that will enable the reader to understand more readily what took place

When I first saw Hugh, he was being carried on a stretcher into the house in Westminster where I worked. He had been diagnosed as suffering from advanced tuberculosis with severe cavitation of the lungs. He was far too weak to walk. He had come at the suggestion of his general practitioner for a consultation with Mr F. Matthias Alexander, the originator of the Alexander Technique. It was a last despairing hope so far as he was concerned.

Against all the odds, he experienced a remission of his symptoms and, with Alexander's help, learnt to employ the technique. Indeed, he recovered from his sickness, the cavitation healed and he was able to return to his work as a mining engineer and resume a normal life.

This happy state of affairs lasted for seven years, after which he had to go to Africa again, which necessitated the usual vaccinations, including one against smallpox. It was known that this might involve some risk, but he was assured by his consultant that it was negligible. However, no sooner had he set foot on African soil than he knew that the symptoms had reappeared. He speedily completed his work and returned to England as fast as possible.

By this time Alexander was no longer alive, so it was to me that he turned for help. We worked together intensively once more and eventually the cavitation healed a second time; whereupon he was able to resume a normal life.

This story must seem highly improbable on the face of it, although it is recognised that remissions do sometimes occur in such cases. But this was in the days before there was satisfactory drug treatment, and spontaneous recovery with healing of cavitation was highly unusual. Bed rest, clean air and a sound diet were the usual prescription, with avoidance of all strenuous activity and excessive demand upon the breathing mechanism. But the prognosis was pessimistic.

So what bearing could Hugh's involvement with Mr F. Matthias Alexander, and his eponymous technique, possibly have had upon the course of his illness and his subsequent recovery? As he tells in the story, he was evidently in no doubt about the answer. He considered that it was to this that he owed his life.

People who know little or nothing about these things may well be sceptical, but here are some facts to take into consideration. F. Matthias Alexander was an aspiring actor (born in Tasmania in 1869) who had succeeded in helping himself overcome severe difficulties with his breathing and use of voice. He had evolved a practical technique that he first taught to other voice users so that they might help themselves. At that period there was a considerable amount of tuberculosis in Australia, particularly in the big cities, and the accepted treatment, as previously mentioned, emphasised the importance of placing a minimal demand upon the breathing mechanism, so as to avoid spreading the infection further throughout the lungs. This view was quite the contrary to Alexander's own experience and observation. He believed that full, unimpeded, natural breathing was an essential requirement for the human organism, and that sufferers from respiratory deficit need to breathe more efficiently so that a proper use of the lungs can enable the healing power of Nature to take its effect. He argued this case very strongly and convinced, by means of practical demonstration, a number of experienced and eminent medical men - first in Australia and then in London - that his view was correct. So it came about that his technique began to be adopted and increasingly practised.

The discovery he had made was the fact that our breathing habits are intimately bound up with our postural mechanism: that the entire functioning of the human organism is bound up with the mechanisms of balance and posture that make possible our human bipedal existence. The way in which we use ourselves not only to stand, sit, walk and move, but also to think, reason, feel and react to stimuli, profoundly affects our breathing, circulation and digestion. And the way that we do all these things needs to be carefully regulated by conscious control and awareness to ensure that habits of misuse are obviated and that natural healthy functioning prevails.

This was the Technique that Hugh so painstakingly learnt and put into practice. Later, he experienced one more slight setback; but by then an efficient drug treatment had been discovered and in the end, by virtue of his remarkable courage and perseverance, this story was able to reach a happy conclusion.

Walter Carrington
April 2000

PREFACE

Hugh Massey was a man whose charm, natural intelligence and determination took him a long way from his humble origins. Born in London's East End in 1914, he was brought up in Nottingham from the age of 10 and attended Nottingham High School. His father was a sailor and he had relatively little contact with him due to his long absences at sea. Also, his mother died when he was only 15. Hugh's later career was often beset with difficulties and setbacks, but his ability to respond so positively to the challenges life presented to him was a tribute to his fortitude and optimism. He was the quintessential self-made man and above all he was a survivor.

When he found himself in the Free French colony of Cameroon in West Africa during the Second World War, he had little idea that the ground was being laid for a personal research project which was to preoccupy him for most of his life. The combination of his observation of African wild life - great apes in particular - and his contact with different sections of the local African population came to take on an unexpected new perspective when he found himself the victim of TB. Such was the seriousness of his condition - in the days before new drug technology made the breakthrough in the treatment of this devastating disease - that he was considered effectively to have been given a death sentence. Seemingly by chance, but in Hugh's view by destiny, he happened to come across the theories of F.M.Alexander, which offered him a faint ray of hope in his desperate situation. The extraordinary cure he was able to effect through this unorthodox approach led him to some radical conclusions concerning human evolution. In his view, the key to understanding the ascent of man lay in the matter of posture. Significantly, this was the lynchpin of Alexander's whole theory of health and well being, as embodied in his internationally regarded Alexander Technique.

Hugh Massey's chance encounter with a band of pygmies in the hinterland of Cameroon - of a kind whose characteristics are significantly different from the mainstream pygmy population – was the experience that was to give him the starting-point for his idea. He came to believe that the emergence of man came not via the great apes but through varieties of monkey with particular characteristics, and that the pygmy holds an important place in this development. However, it is important to recognise that Hugh was not singling out the African pygmy in this respect. The cornerstone of his theory was based on the realisation that until relatively recent times the whole Equatorial belt had been home to pygmoid peoples, nearly all of whom had disappeared. He concluded that this population as a whole had been the transitional element in the evolutionary emergence of man. Only through particular geographic conditions has pygmy survival been exclusive to Africa in our own times and it was precisely the environmental conditions on the Equator that allowed this evolutionary transition. He quite reasonably surmised, on the basis of the notable difference in height, colour and build between the mainstream local pygmy population and the group that he had encountered in the forests of Cameroon, that pygmy populations worldwide had grown taller. Moreover, this had happened over a surprisingly short period of time; a fact supported by specialised anthropological research. Pygmies had also been disappearing to a significant extent through miscegenation with the local population.

The remarkable fact about Hugh Massey's thesis, which he began to develop in outline in the late 1940s, is that at the present time, 50 to 60 years later, certain parallels seem to be emerging between his ideas and the work of respected mainstream scientists. Such an eminent geneticist as Luka Cavalli-Sforza of Stanford University argues, on the basis of DNA analysis, that the pygmies are probably our oldest human ancestor.* Similarly, Owen Lovejoy of Case Western University has focused in on posture as a significant factor in human evolution, in a number of his research papers.

Hugh's account of his experiences and research in *An African Odyssey* make it a unique combination of elements, genre-wise. It is at one and same time, a travel book, an autobiography, an account of the efficaciousness of an unorthodox therapeutic approach and a theory of human evolution. The resulting structure of the book, which has been preserved editorially, was entirely appropriate to the author's individuality, breadth of experience and wide-ranging interests.

Hugh Massey was above all an adventurer by nature, physically and intellectually. A man of natural humanity, courage and optimism, he was always open to new ideas and prepared to take chances both existentially and intellectually. I met him in the last few years of his life when he was in his late 60s. He died at the age of 79 in 1994 and will not be easily forgotten by those who knew him. He inspired both strong affection and occasional antagonism. If *An African Odyssey* appears controversial or provocative in its thrust, that would undoubtedly have pleased Hugh. Above all he had the virtue of being a perfectly genuine person who was not one to tell you what he thought you wanted to hear.

John Adler
July 2000

---

* *The History and Geography of Human Genes* by Luka Cavalli-Sforza. Co-authors: Menozzi and Piazza (Princeton University Press).

CHAPTER 1

From the verandah of my bungalow looking across the valley towards the old administration quarters, one can see a cluster of apricot-washed, colonial buildings, with red tiled roofs and hibiscus-clad walls. Elegant and slightly withdrawn, they stand in a little grove of eucalyptus trees. We are in Yaounde in the French Cameroons. These buildings were first erected by the German Government before the First World War. Now in the custodianship of the colonial French administration, they have lasted 30 or 40 years with scarcely any outward change. Each has a placard denoting its function: *Chef de Région, Bureaux des Finances, Chef de Subdivision, Le Palais de Justice, Département des Eaux et Forêts.* They have a flavour of old German architecture, such as is glimpsed from a railway train when journeying through the Black Forest, only here they are weathered by years of tropical sun and rain. Slightly to the left of this group, in splendid imperial isolation, stands the *Palais du Gouverneur* with an occupied sentry box on either side of the drive up to the palace. The imposing main gates hide an impressive ornamental garden, with well-tended lawns and tropical flowers.

The view across the valley from the residence of the Governor and his wife is of a town laid out before the advent of motor transport. It is a typical African town: dusty red laterite roads, a straggle of tin-roofed shacks and shops. Here and there a hint of a better building emerges, which tells of a slow evolution from old-style trading post into a shanty town with modest aspirations towards sophistication.

The development of the town can be seen in other ways. Scales and weighing balances stand like gibbets in front of Greek- and Syrian-owned stores, ready for hanging the bags of produce which the local natives bring daily for sale. Cocoa beans, palm kernels, tins of pressed palm-tree oil, beniseed, firewood, plaited raffia mats - all these products are carried on the heads of the native women who make up the majority of the local population, for sale to the traders. All bagged produce is bought and sold in kilograms, and the early morning hubbub of haggling over price and quality makes for an unmistakable African sound. Each morning, except Sunday, when the mission stations require the presence of the natives, little groups of men and women begin their walk into town. They begin early, before the tropical sun reaches its zenith and makes everyone hot and listless, for although we are 3,000 feet above sea level we are only 4 degrees north of the Equator.

Distance to these people seems of little account. They walk easily, even when loaded up with market produce, and some travel 30 or 40 miles on foot in the day preceding the morning market, so as to arrive in good time. They always travel barefoot with liana and raffia-plaited baskets or round enamel basins filled to the brim, balanced carefree and insouciantly on their heads. Women from these areas dress plainly, in black cotton dresses or simply printed cotton skirts and frocks made in Manchester. There is no indigenous costume, such as one sees in Northern Nigeria or in the Islamic lands to the north, where the women are highly colourful by comparison, with their bright robes and elaborate headscarves. Hereabouts, native people dress in poor imitation of the Europeans, although the men sometimes wear black or white singlets above a wrap-around waist-high print. Hairstyles are short, either shaved close to the skull or, for women, in little screw knots which they spend much time in elaborating.

The Second World War, which is presently in progress, has slowed up many of the developments in lifestyle that are already overdue in this little township. But even so, new economic and political undercurrents are seeping through and one senses that we are living in the midst of impending yet barely identifiable change. At a practical level, lorries are coming into the town in ever-increasing numbers, bringing the tropical produce by which the country leads its economic life, since crops are now being gathered together in remoter areas deeper and deeper into the hinterland beyond Yaounde, and these trucks are bringing them direct to collecting stores and companies in Yaounde.

I am General Manager of one of those companies, British-owned, which dates back into the remote past of colonial expansion into West Africa. Yaounde has been the site of a company station for many years, predating the German administration before the First World War when the interior of the Cameroons was but a large space on the map with very little detail. We are the main town inland, lying at the head of the largely single-track railway system, which is our only practical means of transportation to the shipping port. Built by the Germans, this railway is a minor marvel of engineering in difficult terrain, passing through heavily forested rain-drenched lands, across fast-flowing rivers and through steamy, mosquito-infested swamps and valleys. Wood is plentiful and is used to fuel the locomotives, so that the little trains are heralded by plumes of smoke as they thread their way up the altitude. Enormous sections cut from huge tropical trees form the substance of culvers and bridges, whilst viaducts and landslip faces are made from steel and stone. Imported steel structures are employed for the major rivers, such as at the crossing over the wide and powerful Sanaga.

CHAPTER 2

Today, as on most fine mornings, I have breakfast served on the verandah. The sun is already well up and the garden boys are working away at cutting the lawn with their home-made scythes fashioned from strips of steel hoop taken from bales. The lawns are trim and neat and watered every day in the dry season. The flower gardens round the house are filled with bright tropical and subtropical plants, mixed with rose bushes brought from England. Roses wear themselves out here, blooming three times a year and surrendering their scent in the effort of excessive profusion. The grounds are surrounded by a high hibiscus hedge and, in the shady patches away from the main drive, expatriate European vegetables hide under little cloches of palm leaves. Like American tobacco, most of our plants are shade grown under leaves which the gardeners cut from the ubiquitous oil palms at the roadside. In this way they are able to pass the noonday heat under protection.

Waiting for my driver to arrive and take me to the office, I think spasmodically about the day's work ahead. Usually, it is rather dull: reports to the company HQ back home in Liverpool; financial summaries of the month's results and forecasting the next; indenting for new supplies against a war-regulated background which governs everything we are able to import from England or America. But despite the War and the sense of isolation it generates, life as a 28-year-old English bachelor in a French colonial community has many compensations. No matter what the restrictions may be on food supplies - and they are not usually anything more serious than flour rationing - the French have a wonderful ability to produce good food under almost any circumstances, no matter where they are. They blanch a little when invited to dinner by a solitary Englishman who is restricted to the small repertoire of a cook whose training has been confined to serving roast chicken at every opportunity and making the eternal banana fritters for dessert.

French administrators, army officers and trade employees are often blessed with French wives who produce mouth-watering dishes for the little elegant dinner parties we create for each other. Because we are fortunate in enjoying an ample resource of domestic staff for housework and food preparation, entertaining is easier and more frequent than would be possible in a similar community in Europe. We whites comprise a mere 2,000 souls or so, living for the most part in comfort and security among a native population for whom domestic service with a European household generally carries enviable status.

I employ eight servants, or 'boys': a head boy, Vincent; a houseboy, Sixpence; a chauffeur, Stephen; a cook - no name, as cooks tend to come and go in dismal procession once their limitations are exposed to the ruthless gaze of French ladies who know about these things; a head gardener, Joseph; two labourers for general work and a kitchen boy to fetch wood, clean dishes and tend the fires. The dense equatorial forest is only some 60 miles to the west of us, down the hills which slope towards the coast, and to have the small luxury of an English-style fireplace is a rare and slightly exotic privilege. For in the rainy season, especially in areas near to streams and rivers, the nights become cool and clammy, not unlike those chill and moist autumn evenings in England.

Vincent comes to call me. He has been my personal boy ever since I came to Yaounde three years ago, following an earlier stint in the insufferable, grinding climate of coastal Douala. Yaounde is a blessed relief, with a healthy drier climate and the small-town community with its peculiar atmosphere of gossip, scandal, cultural activity and good conversation. Moreover, Yaounde is the jumping-off point for travel to the vast and fascinating interior, stretching unimaginable distances eastwards across the whole wide belt of Africa. One day, perhaps, I will be able to set off and do some exploring in territory off the road. The farthest I have travelled east is to Bafia, which takes the greater part of a day and involves crossing a major river. One of my friends was crossing last year on the Bac and two or three hippos came under the ferry and tried to upset it. But experiences like that are not commonplace and desk-bound workers like myself rarely get out into the farthermost reaches of this fascinating and little-known land.

On my way to the office, I always call at the Post Office to collect the mail and Vincent has just told me in the *lingua franca* of pidgin English that we all use: "Massa, motua he done come." Stephen, my driver, is punctual and always clean and smart in his white drill uniform and chauffeur's cap. No matter how dusty the roads have made the car in our previous day's travel, my Chevrolet saloon is always clean and smart when I am picked up in the morning. Indeed, it is the envy of most of the other Europeans. The mail has to be collected *en route* to the office from our private mailbox, which lies directly below the bungalow. I alone have the key, since the mail often contains documents or money for the company for which, as General Manager, I am *'le responsable'*, as the French say.

On this particular day, there is a letter which, although I do not know it, is of importance not only to my company, but to me personally. Something of its contents had been hinted at in a recent telephone conversation, but always we are wary of saying too much on the phone, for this is wartime. There may be spies - certainly there are Frenchmen with leanings towards the Vichy government who are not friendly to us - and so we are guarded in our phone conversations and keep discussion of any subject such as vessel loadings and movements of produce to ourselves. The Post Office is a recognised meeting-place for us Europeans as we collect our mail. There is one passenger train each day from the port, which arrives in the evening and which makes early morning letter collection a pleasant necessity. It enables us all to shake hands with friends and acquaintances, to exchange morning greetings and news and generally to indulge in small-town affabilities. Rather like buying bread in a Parisian baker's shop, it is a little ceremony which creates a context for the sharing of rumours as well as ameliorating the concealed disquiet that underlies our common expatriate condition.

"Good morning Felix, good morning Alfred," is my standard greeting to the bookkeepers as I pass through the office into the inner sanctum where I have my desk. They always stand up as I pass through - part of the daily civility and a relaxed, respectful gesture which says in effect: 'You are the Boss. We know of no other greeting for you as we have been trained by years of office discipline to behave like this. But we do so with smiles and even, on occasion, with a little submerged affection. But sometimes, too, a little hostility, if salary raises have not been finalised or if criticism of our work has rankled.'

The confidential letter is from Head Office in Liverpool. It sets out the circumstances of a new project which, because I am located in Yaounde, falls necessarily to me and deals with the issue of wild rubber. Now that Malaya has fallen and synthetic rubber production at home has problems, I am required to co-operate with the Free French government officials in a programme for stimulating alternative production, arranging finance and managing the collection of all the wild rubber that can be obtained. It is not to take up all my time, but I am required to report regularly and quickly on prospects, and state how I propose to tackle the scheme.

The first person I shall see is not an official but Monsieur Brouillet, a Frenchman who lives just down the road from my bungalow and has a transport-cum-merchanting business. I've had a few dealings with him in the past. He's also transacted small parcels of wild rubber and he knows the areas where it can be found growing. Brouillet is very commercially minded, energetic, and could be a useful ally. He is pro-De Gaulle, which fuels the optimism of many who might otherwise give way to despondency about the fall of France and the collaborationist Vichy government. I shall also try to get the higher-grade administration officials to support the scheme.

Brouillet has a nice, modern, airy concrete bungalow, built by his own staff, with the usual small garden and white cement-washed verandah. Inside, polished concrete floors make for cool living in the hottest periods, and the customary coverings of hand-woven carpets, mats and locally made furniture have an air of simplicity and rugged honesty about them. Brouillet is no intellectual and there are precious few books around; only bookcases filled with imitation book covers carrying titles of the classics, which deceives no one. I come straight to the point with Brouillet. I tell him that this is something we can all do to help the war effort, which is self-evidently true and I ask for his co-operation. We sit down to cold beer and begin talking.

"What do you feel is the best way of getting really substantial rubber production going, Monsieur Brouillet? I have firm instructions to buy. I shall, of course, go to the palace and they will help, I am sure." Brouillet looks appraisingly at me and asks, "How much are you prepared to pay?" I weave in and out of the negotiations, saying price depends on quality and quantity and where it has to be delivered. "Don't worry about transport," he says, "I have the trucks and they go into the interior anyway, to Bertoua and Batouri. I have an administration contract to deliver drums of petrol and oil. No one will be able to give a better service than I can, because I can bring the rubber back on the return journey."

This is doubtless true, but it is putting the cart before the horse. We shall have to get the production immeasurably increased before we need to talk logistics. I then point out that, before the First World War, the Germans obtained a lot of wild rubber from numbers of forest areas and we shall need to look closely at the possibilities of doing likewise. We are conscious that we are now 30 years further on than the old-timers.

Brouillet brings the conversation back to immediate practicality by saying, "We are talking of Yokadouma; that's where any real tonnage has to come from. You can't expect to achieve much overnight, and don't expect too much to come from talking to top brass. They won't buy it, or handle it, or finance it. They won't do the work. They can help and no doubt will, but theirs is just talk - necessary talk, but not action. So I ask you again, how much money are we talking about? Or are we talking about goods in exchange?

"So much of the economy of those areas depends on things other than money - things like salt and fish-hooks, cloth, machetes, baling strip. Some of those are a bit hard to come by, as we both know; salt especially." He continues: "I think you will best attract enthusiasm if you can obtain from England extra supplies which we can then use to stimulate production."

Poor England, fighting for its survival. Sailors, risking their lives just to bring salt in bags and fish-hooks and blankets through waters made perilous in the extreme by enemy submarines and surface raiders; all to sell to natives who know almost nothing of the war in Europe and who are blissfully free of its dangers.

In the final count, our plans for rubber production involve getting the numbers worked out and convincing the administration of the need. Logistical problems of transport, purchasing, quality inspection, payment, could all be left to the thrust of commerce. Apart from Brouillet, there are several Greek and Syrian traders who have experience of buying and selling produce to the main companies. But as buyers on behalf of the Ministry of Supply in London, we need to develop what has until now been a sporadic trade and to make it into a regular and dependable activity.

Working out the numbers - the basis for the buying price, the quality premium, the penalty for inferior material, the weighing and inspection, the delivery to Yaounde and the storage and collection for shipment to the UK - are all within my experience. But first we have to get the administration machine to move and here, as elsewhere, such matters are best discussed over a meal or a drink. I contact the Governor's aide and invite him to my home. Like so many of the Free French at this time, he is helpful and approachable. The peacetime distinctions between government officials and 'trade' have been greatly reduced, especially towards Englishmen, who are a very rare breed in the colony these days. In the time I have been here I have already been invited to sit on the petrol rationing committee and the Red Cross local body, and to take a share in price control consultative work. And so the new venture to promote rubber is easily developed in principle. We agree that administration shall give out the necessary policy directives to the *Chefs de Région*, who will in turn pass them on to their subdivisions. The man in Yokadouma, whom I have met several times when he has come into Yaounde, will be central to the success of the project, and I decide to write him a little personal note. It takes a letter four or five days to reach Yokadouma, and therefore it is a rather agreeable surprise to receive a telegram within a short time saying, "Delighted to do everything I can. Can you come yourself in about two months' time? Please bring case of Johnny Walker, regards, Tourmente."

And so we set in train the various steps towards a programme. I ask Liverpool to send quantities of the various goods we will need to stimulate enthusiasm among the rubber gatherers who live in the distant forests, of which Ituri is the largest and the least explored in the region.

CHAPTER 3

Liverpool Head Office is marvellous. What employee located abroad normally says that of his management at home? In a very short time they have got together the goods we need and secured the shipping priorities for their release. Tourmente, for his part, has been able to call together all the local chiefs of the various tribes, and has waved the big stick to the effect that they have to help the white man's war against the Germans. Some of them, let it be said, still retain the most affectionate memories of the German administration, but the message gets home. Woe betide those who do not pull their weight, says Tourmente, and he sets them production targets for each area which means they will have to work hard, very hard. The mixture of flattery, cajolery, persuasion and downright intimidation brings forth a crop of forecast figures which are relayed to me as monthly projections for planning purposes. They are so good that I immediately halve them before passing them on to management in Liverpool. One has learned by experience that initial enthusiasms are liable soon to be tempered in the enervating climate, and hazards are often underestimated. But at any rate, we have got off to a good start.

Everyone pulls their weight and decision-making progresses in an untrammeled and free-wheeling atmosphere. Until, that is, the day a month or so later when Brouillet comes into my office and says: "I need more money. I can't go all that way to buy what I hear is soon coming into the market unless I have more cash." The old fox! But money has to be found for everyone and such is the willingness to help that Harry, my superior in the company, authorises it within two or three days. Commerce in wartime smoothes so many paths whilst at one and the same time it erodes or even destroys traditional values. The cash authorisation comes and I collect large packets of notes from the bank, draw up the documents for signature and prepare to receive the first major consignment of rubber from the anticipated market.

And now, there is an anticlimax. Predictably, people are not behaving as they should. Rumour reaches me that Tourmente has already lost his initial enthusiasm. The Catholic Church is protesting at the disturbance in family life the rubber gatherers are having to endure; some traders are cheating on the price and paying less than they should and the native chiefs are getting resentful at the criticism they are receiving. These are early days, it is true. The planned increases have yet to be translated from figures on paper into practical achievement. But goods are arriving from England and finding their way rapidly to the areas of production. I remember Tourmente's request to take him a case of whisky and, although it is a few months later than we initially arranged, I decide to go to Yokadouma myself and talk things over with the *Chef de Région* and Tourmente on the spot. The scotch whisky will be used as a means of lubricating a satisfactory response to the market's under-production to date.

I send a telegram to Bertoua and Yokadouma - allowing the three days needed to reach my friend Tourmente - and announce that, finally, I will be with him in a week's time - definitely. I even announce the imminent arrival of the case of whisky - an event which is a minor miracle in itself, as whisky is like gold dust. I give instructions to the staff: tell the houseboys they can have a week off and arrange to lock the safe, the house and the garage.

The early mornings at this time of year are a sheer delight. There is a nip in the air and all the flowers look cool and fresh. At 6am we are off, empty kerosene boxes packed with food and drink for the journey, the luggage stowed away. Stephen, excused from wearing his white drill chauffeur's uniform, is rigged out in khaki shirt and shorts.

In reality, the distance is not great; but it is a tiring journey over laterite roads, for there is scarcely a stretch of hard metal road in the whole of the country. Our route to Yokadouma will be via Bertoua. All the wonderful variety of African vegetation is to be seen on this journey: the tall, tough elephant grasses of the plains, the orchard-covered hills with their round, worn contours made soft and hazy by small bushes and clusters of trees, and then finally the beginnings of the great primeval forest which blankets vast areas of East Cameroon, the Congo and Equatorial Africa.

I call at the *Chef de Région's* office in Bertoua and meet the Administrator for a few moments. He seems vaguely bored by the subject of rubber collection but, in fairness, he has plenty of other claims upon his attention in the administration of the large remote territory which his area covers. We go on and gradually the forest closes in on the narrow road, which is wide enough for two vehicles to pass each other only if both slow down to skirt the deep drainage ditches that are vital to keep the track safe in the rainy season. Virgin Africa lies within a few yards of the car on either side of us, lonely, filled with vast trees stilled by the heat of the windless day and trailing their creeper vines and lianas down to the floor. We cross wooden bridges spanning culverts and forest streams, which are no more than two stout planks on timber supports. It is a silent, soporific track of a road. But suddenly, as we slow down, an excited shout from Vincent and Stephen rouses me. There, not 10 metres from the car, stands a huge lumbering full-grown male gorilla. Both the boys are terrified. And I pretend not to be. I even make a joke about him being there just to check our driving papers. He stands motionless as we drive slowly by. Part of me wants to prolong a sighting which, by any standard, is an unusual experience. Part of me wishes to get away through the fear that large animals in the African wild seem to arouse. I am fairly comfortable with captive animals, for I have five caged chimpanzees in my garden in Yaounde as well as a young leopard. But the sudden impact of being confronted in the wild, without a rifle, by a monster of a creature makes me feel understandably unsafe. As it happens, there is no need to have a gun because in a few seconds we are off, leaving him to move in slow majestic tempo back into his tree cover.

CHAPTER 4

It is nearly dusk when we arrive in Yokadouma. Tourmente is there to welcome me and to show me into the spare bedroom in his house. Usually, visitors to this little town are expected to put themselves up in one of the *Gites D'Etape* - government rest houses set apart for European travellers in many of the remoter areas of the territory. A bath, a change of clothes, the customary glass of whisky filled to the brim with water - we drink long in these parts - and we settle in to the pleasantries. Tourmente wants to know about what is really happening in the war, as though I have inside knowledge denied to the general public. I tell him how I'd gone home to England in 1940 and lived through the news of the Dunkirk evacuation, seen the operation of rationing and driven at night without lights. But I have no tales of personal hardship or actual danger to relate. Even though, on my second wartime voyage, I'd sailed back during a month which saw some of the heaviest losses to the merchant fleet in the whole of the war, I'd seen no enemy action. Tourmente tells me he has had no news of his family, who are somewhere in the South of France, and I suddenly feel that he has much more to bear than I. He tells me that he did not even know about the outbreak of the war until three days after the declaration. Here he is, in this remote township with no other resident European for company, with a radio that breaks down quite often and cut off from news of family and friends who are still in occupied Europe.

He has made the best of his situation. Dinner is a little masterpiece, *coq au vin* with all the fine full flavours of Bordeaux cooking, and followed by delicious sweets, fine cheese and coffee. How typically French to have maintained their standard of culinary excellence in so remote and modest a household on the edge of the Ituri Forest. In addition, Tourmente has come to terms with his loneliness in other ways, as two giggling young and comely black girls hover in the area of the back room.

Tourmente is in very good form. As soon as dinner is over, he tells me he has invited one or two of the Greek traders to come and have coffee. Brouillet has also said he will join us. Tourmente goes on to tell us how he had called meetings with the chiefs and told them he was most dissatisfied with their results. Jokingly - or was it? - he says that he has threatened to smack their bottoms if things do not improve. Given the memories of some of the chiefs, who know very well from First World War days what a beaten bottom feels like - for the Germans were firm disciplinarians - he now knows that there has been a notable response. Pacing up and down the little room under the big old-fashioned ceiling fan turning the sticky air, Tourmente is centre stage. In his excitement and perhaps inflated by a third glass of whisky, he forecasts the biggest rubber market we have ever seen. Of course, we all know that at best it will only be a few hundred tonnes, but we purr our satisfaction. The Greeks and Syrians know that they will buy most of it, for they are the best traders. With jokes and smiles they wheedle the native women into selling to them rather than run the gauntlet of the competing scales at the adjoining stalls. The chances are that they will get a lower price than if they had shown greater confidence in the free-market system prevailing, but will perhaps go away happy with an extra few beads or a fish-hook given gratis and in addition.

Tourmente tells how the news has been spread throughout the forest. Some of the natives bringing the loads have travelled long distances, walking the forest paths for days. I am about to raise the question of quality control when the traders are announced. Soon, the little room is filled and Tourmente surveys the largest gathering he has ever hosted since he came to Yokadouma. Drinks all round. Some of the Syrians are teetotal and sit embarrassed on the edge of their chairs, for they rarely have the chance to sit socially with a French government official. But there is nonetheless an air of excitement. To lower the temperature I say that I am not sure whether some of the produce will be good enough. We know that the natives have only the most primitive methods of coagulating their rubber sap.

Brouillet enters the discussion: "Don't you worry about all that Mr. Massey, they know what they can use. If they can't find formic acid, it will be their own piddle they'll use and I've sold you tonnes of piddle-cured rubber which you never knew about." Everyone laughs. But they don't know that I've had stern instructions from England to watch out for sticky rubber, which is improperly coagulated, and also to penalise for stones, dirt, leaves and general contaminants. I say as much and one can see the little mental calculations going on for the adjustments they will have to make as they buy.

Brouillet seems confident of his part in the show. I would not put it past him to have cornered a little area, perhaps by getting a promise in advance from some chiefs to sell exclusively to him.

Conversation turns to other things. As the only Englishman in the gathering and one of the few who has been to England and returned since the fall of France, I am deemed to know more than most. But of course, my day-to-day news has the same origin as theirs - the BBC Overseas Service, broadcasting the Free French messages and news. We speculate on how effective some of those cryptic 'Jean loves Michelle' kind of messages really are. Our little band of mixed nationalities in this remote corner of the forest feels immensely withdrawn from that great conflict. We have no contact with it, and no imagination is great enough to comprehend the worldwide drama being played out thousands of miles away. If the truth is told, most of us are partly relieved not to be any nearer. Better far to be brave at a remove where we cannot imagine actual danger from guns or air raids. No plane has ever flown over these areas and locally the last guns were silenced well before the Armistice of 1918.

The conversation changes direction again, bringing it nearer to home. I tell them of the sighting of the full-grown male gorilla by the roadside and have the satisfaction of hearing them say that, despite many trips through this part of Africa over many years, none of them has ever had the luck to see a gorilla in the wild. We then listen to Tourmente repeating his account of how the market day tomorrow has been organised. We now learn that to make sure that the natives have a fair chance of selling their produce to whom they please, he has barred the road until the market actually begins. Two of his native staff have been instructed to erect a barrier at each end of the single dirt track, which is the main street, along which stand the shacks and little shops with their corrugated iron roofs. In front of each buying point stands a classical Roman balance. There are even one or two diminutive platform scales in addition, brought all the way from Yaounde. Heaped up beside them are white bags of salt, one of the currencies of exchange. Alongside are the trestles, which carry the bush country wares laid out for sale.

In some ways open-air markets are the same everywhere, except that there are no canopies or elaborate stalls here. Tourmente's plan is for us all to be there at 6.30 in the morning to see the opening of the market. The Syrians have already strolled down the road and noted that none of the natives bringing produce is yet in the main street, which is almost deserted. And so expectancy is in the air, rather as when one waits for the curtain to go up at the start of an evening of theatre.

Tourmente is indeed something of a theatre manager. In the morning he and I swallow a quick coffee and leave the administration house to go into the market. A government pickup, with two black soldiers in uniform, stands waiting for us. They are regulars of the handful of locally recruited military personnel, who are always in attendance to guard government officers. Tourmente and I get in the cab. The soldiers climb into the back with their rifles and bugles, and we drive off slowly down towards the market area. At the first sight of the pickup, a huge shout goes up from the scores of groups of natives.

Suddenly all is bustle, noise, confusion and hurried activity as the loads are picked up and everyone surges towards the barriers. At first, only our pickup is allowed through a barrier, which like the gate at a railway level crossing is lifted to point an authoritative finger to the sky. We drive slowly down the almost empty road, from the first barrier to the second at the other end of the track. This track goes on for a few yards into the edge of the forest and then peters out into a surface only wide enough for walkers or cyclists. We turn and go back again; all is in order and the produce buyers are ready in front of their shops and stalls.

Tourmente gives the order and the soldiers pick up their bugles and give a joyous blast. Fancifully, perhaps, I hear it as if it were the tally-ho of an English fox-hunting call to hounds. At once the barriers are raised and the crowds of natives surge with their loads of produce into the market street, making the hubbub which crowds all over the world produce when busy and involved. Soon, the crowd thins as they split into groups visiting the small shops and stalls. Some are delighted, bemused in a few cases by the unfamiliar feeling of having so much money in their hands. They visit the places which offer the goods they want and enjoy the special feeling of being courted by shopkeepers and buyers who sell them little articles and trinkets as well as the staple foods and clothing. Perhaps I should mention that most of the people who have come to sell their produce are naked but for small coverings of the genitals. Local town folk are easily distinguished, for they wear printed cotton skirts or Japanese-manufactured singlets and trousers. But the great majority are unclothed, without shoes; free and simply uninhibited. For the most part they are pygmies.

CHAPTER 5

Although, the natives of Cameroon are shorter in stature than most of the Africans to be found in the main towns in the west of the country, it is easy to distinguish pygmies from the various types of people originating hereabouts. For one thing they are shorter. But pygmies are unmistakably different in general appearance. I am quite used to seeing them walk past my bungalow in Yaounde along the road from Akonolinga, an area which contains a population of pygmies that has been studied for many years. But this is the first time I have seen so many pygmies together, and they are clearly different from those I have seen elsewhere. These in Yokadouma are smaller than those I have seen in Yaounde. Whilst pygmies do vary between groups, those we see in Yokadouma have hair which is different, as is their general facial appearance. By now, some of them look a little less happy than in the euphoric moments when the market began. Perhaps they have worked out the balance between the the worth of the goods relative to the cash they have received in return, in the light of the the hard and at times perilous experience of gathering in the forest plus the effort of the long journey to market; to all of which must be added the task of preparing the finished strips of rubber.

By 9.30am, with the sun already heating up and the feeling that breakfast would be a good idea, we think about returning to Tourmente's house. There seems to be little more for us to do at present. All the rubber has been sold and the market is virtually at an end. Lorry drivers begin to supervise loading the bundles of rubber and other produce into the trucks. By noon, the whole exercise will have been completed and after lunch I will go straight back home to Yaounde. So we turn the pickup round, the soldiers climb aboard and we go for a final trip down the little road through the uplifted barrier and drive the short distance towards the place where the road peters out into the forest paths. There are a few very big trees by the roadside, broad-leaved evergreens which afford a large pool of shade around their trunks.

Suddenly we see them - pygmies: somewhere between 15 and 20 people, both men and women, but no children, in a little group sitting together in the shade. It is an arresting sight, for these are not ordinary dark-skinned pygmies of the kind we have just seen in the market-place. They are yellow. We are incredulous, stunned by this totally unfamiliar, unexpected sight. Both Tourmente and I have lived among natives in the Cameroons for years; we have got totally used to seeing all varieties of costume, physique, age, dress and undress. But neither of us has ever seen anything remotely like this. Tourmente stops the truck, the soldiers dismount and we move slowly towards the little group under the tree. We are perhaps 30 metres away from them, but as soon as they see us a minor panic sets in. They hurriedly grab their few possessions and start to move agitatedly away from us. We too are rather scared - too scared for the moment to tell the soldiers with their rifles across their backs to leave us.

Why are we scared? After all, we are accustomed to living permanently outnumbered by natives wherever we travel in the territory and I have never had a moment's fear of them. At this point in the history of Africa, a white skin almost guarantees freedom from harm. For the Africans, among whom we spend our daily lives, are tolerant, submissive people who have respect, either naturally or hierarchically instilled, for the minority of ruling Europeans.

But this is a totally new situation for us, as it is for these primitive people. So in order to defuse any tension inherent in the situation, we stop in our tracks, look pleasant and smile at them. The little group hesitates, jabbering excitedly amongst themselves, but then they decide they are too close to us for comfort and they begin to gather their remaining possessions - spears, bows and arrows, staves and baskets - and move further away. We stand our ground, not wishing to give them more cause for alarm. Now both sides stand still and gaze at each other in perplexity and mutual astonishment. It gives me time to take in their appearance more fully.

First, it dawns on me that never, anywhere, have I seen such small people. Secondly, never have I seen yellow-skinned people in Africa. Thirdly, there is something about their proportions which is different. Is it that their arms are longer than normal, shoulders wider than customary? Certainly their physiognomy is very different from any of the other pygmies we've seen. For their part, they've probably never seen white men, even though French missionaries are generally intrepid travellers, penetrating into the remotest corners of Africa.

What have we to be frightened of? The bows and arrows? A little perhaps. But we are the kind of men who habitually make our way through unexpected situations without revealing a trace of apprehension. We are also accompanied, not far behind, by two armed guards who are standing near the pickup on the roadside. It is almost certain that their rifles are not loaded, although they would have live ammunition in their belts. But we mean no harm to anyone, least of all this little group of folk from another dimension. We make signs to the soldiers to stay where they are, remaining still whilst we advance tentatively so as to see them better at closer quarters. At once, their agitation is renewed and with rapid gestures of hands and shaking their heads they move off together - they seem to flit, rather than walk. By this time other ordinary, dark-skinned familiar pygmies have come up and joined us. Although we cannot talk a word to them either, we ask if there is anyone who can speak to them to tell the curious little folk that we mean no harm. We find a native who calls out to them. Nothing doing; they keep on moving away and in a few more moments they have drifted down the forest path and into the trees. I notice, as they go, that they have dried mud on their legs and feet which is darker than their skin. Usually, mud dries on the skin of blacks from other regions in lighter contrast. The colour of mud is of course quite a crude measure, but it just strikes me, these little people really are different. I guess them to be less than four feet high. I see that they move differently, in the sense that their gestures are quicker than one normally sees. When we were near them, they were of course in an excited and agitated frame of mind. But I notice that they have a way of wagging their heads and talking volubly amongst themselves. That too is a mark of difference, as most Africans have impressively still heads, in that their often spendid physique is accompanied by a stillness, or economy of movement, when they speak.

Tourmente and I leave the area slowly, bemused but seemingly unable to speak to each other about what we've seen. The whole episode has not taken more than 20 or so minutes, but we go back in the pickup to the house silent and reflective. We still have more work to do - evaluating the total tonnage of rubber which has been bought, going over some of the material which has been rejected partly as a result of my comments the previous evening, and talking about the next collective market which will have to be arranged. Soon, the events of the morning recede into memory and we get on with the work of the day.

Hospitable as always and possibly welcoming company as an antidote to his habitual isolation, Tourmente persuades me to defer returning until the next day. Siesta next, for it is very hot, followed by evening drinks and another splendid meal. How do these Frenchmen do it? I too live as a bachelor, with a higher income than Tourmente's, but I never seem able to drum up instant hospitality of the quality now enjoyed by Brouillet, Gaitanos and myself. Gaitanos is another wily old bird, a trader who has made a lot of money. He lives in Akonolinga and so the conversation naturally turns to the group of pygmies.

We ask Gaitanos if he has ever seen yellow-pigmented people

in the Akonolinga area. "No," he says, but he's heard of them. Today, he had been too busy looking after his business to leave the shops where the rubber was being bought, and so he'd not seen anything unusual. Ordinary pygmies are an everyday sight for him. Tourmente then says that he has been in the area for several years and not only has he never seen such a sight before, but he has never even heard of it.

Someone asks, "Why have they come here?" since they do not seem to have entered the market, and "Where are they from?" But it seems, from what Tourmente has already found out, that they are shy and apprehensive. The scenes of the market, the noise, the bustle, the haggling, the sales pitches of the Syrians - all these factors have perhaps made them fearful, so that their produce has been handed in to bolder spirits outside the market areas and taken in on their behalf. They never got into the market-place. They have chosen to make the journey, presumably with other pygmies, but have remained practically out of sight. It was just fortuitous and fortunate that we went along the road, for no reason at all except to see the path leading into the forest and happened upon them.

We are, however, all concerned with business and not anthropology, a subject about which each of us is ignorant. We take refuge in Tourmente's remark, "Today, we stepped back for a few moments into the Stone Age" and leave the subject there, confused and disturbed by our lack of understanding, but dimly conscious that something important has been witnessed. Tourmente does say, however, that as soon as he can he will find out more about these people by talking to chiefs. I am also conscious that I am in danger of being ridiculed if I try to attach too much importance to the experience.

CHAPTER 6

In the morning, after breakfast, as we prepare to leave Tourmente, thanking him for all his help, hospitality and, for my part at least, the shared experiences, my driver brings the houseboy and the car to the house. Just as I am ready to set off, a young French missionary asks if I would mind giving him a lift back to the missionary station. I understand that it is on the way back near Bertoua and of course I am glad to be of service. He enters the car, clad in his long white priest's cassock and tropical topee. I ask him if he sighted the yellow pygmies yesterday, but he ignores the question pointedly and says he would sooner talk about the disruption that this drive to increase wild rubber production is having on his flock. Do I know that chiefs had been cajoled and even threatened? Am I aware that men are having to leave their homes, sometimes for days on end to go into the forest? Do I know how dangerous some of the work is, involving climbing into the tops of great trees and collecting the lianas? Finally, do I know of the total disruption to family life that people like me are causing to the people under his pastoral care? Moreover, do I know that not very long ago, a pygmy fell and broke his leg and died from the injury? In short, do I realise what havoc people like me are creating?

There is an underlying hostile note in this man's voice, possibly a sense of resentment that he is getting his free lift from an Englishman. Perhaps he is one of those French colonials who feel that the war has nothing to do with them, nor with the native peoples within their sphere of influence. I try to tell him of the importance to us, and to those who believe in the rightness of the war against Nazi Germany, of the wild rubber programme. He is so far removed from war news, or involvement in the progress of the war in Europe, that he seems almost unapproachable. However, I do remind myself that if anyone might be able to help me with more knowledge of pygmies, he is quite possibly well situated to do so. I press on, asking him what he thought about Tourmente's remark made the previous evening about Stone Age people, adding my own contribution to the effect that it has occurred to me that Darwin's ideas about the descent of man may be significantly connected to the evidence of these 'little people'.

"Please stop the car at once, Monsieur, and let me out. Rather than listen to such talk, I would sooner walk back to the mission," he says. He is visibly very angry with me. Not only do I support - even encourage - the disruption of his pastoral flock, but I talk about them in blasphemous way. He goes on, albeit not insisting too strongly about continuing the journey on foot: "These are God's children, Monsieur, just as we all are. Talk of the 'descent of man' through apes, which is what I suppose you are referring to, is absolute heresy to me. I love these people, work among them and will do what I can to preserve them from the influence of men such as yourself! The church is powerful in this country." We continue the journey in silence.

The tirade was such that it is a relief to us both when we finally get to his destination and I let him out of the car. He thanks me with scant politeness, his beliefs offended, his face still showing outrage. I am still not able to find out whether he has ever seen yellow pygmies or not and I am now reduced to the situation that only Tourmente and I, of all the Europeans present that day, have paid attention or shown interest in this topic. To me it is all rather disturbing. I know, beyond any possibility of doubt, that I have seen something very unusual. I am also mindful of the fact that, whereas traditionally one has to become an explorer and walk many miles on foot before seeing or experiencing the unusual in Africa, I am at present sitting in a chauffeur-driven Chevrolet saloon. That is as near as I have got to hardship or the perils of exploration.

The journey back to Yaounde, with a brief stop to report to the *Chef de Région* in Bertoua, is shortened for me by my reflections on the trip. It has been an eventful few days. But now I must get back into the daily swing of the office. It is soon apparent that nothing very much has occurred in my absence. A man has been disturbed by the night watchman, seen prowling around the company's premises, but it does not amount to anything. There is a heap of mail and soon the need to get reports, indents and cables off to Head Office fills the days with their customary busy routine. The trip to Yokadouma fades gently into the background of memory, except that it has awakened an interest in me to see the Akonolinga pygmies as they walk past the bunaglow. Of course, as fate would have it none walk by for several weeks, although I am on the look out for them. So is Vincent, who has been instructed to call me if any pygmies walk by the house. I suspect that his day-dreaming may be posited more on the prospects of his buying a wife than in my project. At least he too has seen plenty of the local pygmies, so he is no longer in doubt about their general appearance.

This road that leads by my dwelling is quite a busy thoroughfare. Many small black figures, considerably smaller than the Africans who are my real neighbours, walk up and down it; but although they are small, they are not pygmies. Many must be below five feet tall, but they do not possess pygmy features. It would be good to get hold of some books on the subject, for there have surely been studies on pygmies, negrillos and short-statured natives. But all the books on tribes and races of the area are only to be found in libraries and institutions in Europe. I know of none here, nor do I know of anyone who is technically informed in the subject. But I must not overemphasise my interest. Among our local topics of conversation it arouses scarcely anything above a yawn, for none of us has any expertise and few desire to know more. We are just businessmen.

Some months later, my interest is revived a little by the news that an American anthropologist is coming to town. I soon learn that he is not coming in his professional capacity, but is here to try to ascertain if certain minerals such as tantalite and rutile are available or known to exist. These are raw materials greatly in demand and the procurement agency in Washington has seconded Dr Bascombe to initiate an enquiry into the supply position. As he does not speak French and is obviously feeling rather out on a limb and needing local facilities for getting around, I offer him my bachelor hospitality and am glad when he accepts it. I soon learn that his speciality is Yoruba artifacts and art and that he has come to Yaounde from Nigeria as part of his war service.

I am glad to give him a hand in meeting officials in the mines department, which is located in the old administration buildings, and I become interested in knowing more about the minerals which have brought him here. By dint of translating and reading some of his papers, I quickly acquire a superficial acquaintance with the subject. In the course of conversation, however, the subject of the native peoples of the Cameroons reveals as fascinating a kaleidoscope of races as can be found anywhere in Africa. I tell him of my strange trip to Yokadouma, and especially about the pygmies. At once, he asks me where he can see them for himself. I hesitate. Yokadouma is a long way and, even if he goes there, the probability is that he will see nothing extraordinary. After all, Tourmente has lived several years there and only saw this odd little group on the special day of the great rubber market, which took weeks to round up and collect. I seriously doubt, since he has no reliable connection with them, whether they would be accessible to anyone on a casually organised trip. These doubts I communicated to Bascombe, who becomes sceptical about the whole story. He explains to me that there are no anthropological grounds for believing that pre-primitive people exist today, and in my mind, this small band of fewer than 20 folk are deserving of the description of pre-primitives, although I scarcely know what the word must mean. I face up to the fact that I have made an assumption which engenders disbelief, incredulity, or worse, and - most justifiably - the dismissive reaction based on the fact that this is a technical subject of which I know nothing.

As work pressures edge their way into the time I have for any further study of the question, I am diverted into the activities which are opened up by the search for new minerals. The rubber programme seems to have gone as far as it can, for there is a strict limitation on the amount which can be expected from gathering in the wild. I am directed to concentrate my attention into assisting the search for and the purchase of the two special minerals. Rutile is already in regular production as an established mineral in the Cameroons. It occurs in streams as an alluvial ore which has to be hand-dug and panned. Some of the rutile crystals are very big, appearing as lumps up to three or four inches across. In peacetime, it had a small but regular trade with England for use in pottery glazes in Stoke-on-Trent since it fires to a rich brown colour when used as a staining material on earthenware. But in wartime it has acquired a much more significant application. It is one of the compounds used in the production of smokescreens for destroyers, so any increase in production is to be valued.

More and more my work takes me to parts of the hinterland I've never previously visited. Nanga Eboka, itself a pygmy area, contains an abundance of streams in which rutile has been leached from rocks. I go there to look at some of the workings, but I see no pygmies. In fact, the only ones I come across are when, a few months later, a little procession passes by my own front door, carrying an old man who is seated on a chair slung between two poles, carried on the shoulders of four men. The old man is ill, but by the beating of drums and xylophones and the dancing which is being performed ahead of the little band, I can see he is considered important. I first tell Vincent to go into the road and find out where the procession is going. He returns with the message that they are taking their chief to hospital for an operation and I leave the bungalow to see them pass. It is still early in the day and they have come from beyond Akonolinga, so they must have walked for days previously. I stand and watch them for the few minutes it takes them to pass the drive. I wonder what it is that makes pygmies so distinguishable from the local people around me. These are ordinary pygmies - dark-skinned, sometimes around five feet tall, as I estimate, with screwed, tufted hair and occasionally a wispy tuft of beard. I wonder whether their distinguishable characteristic, other than their small stature, is not in the way they move - their gait, their vivacity, their gesticulations. Of course they are in an excited mood, now having in view the town they have travelled so far and so arduously to visit. Moreover, they are celebrating what is for them a significant event. But they do move about with more animation than one normally sees - when suddenly, a possible explanation occurs to me.

In these parts, as in so many areas of West Africa, Negroes carry almost everything on their heads. Pygmies never seem to do so. When I first came to Africa, I was struck by the prevalence of head-portering, but after years of seeing it every day I have ceased to find it remarkable.

Sometimes one sees amusing and surprising examples of the way that our local inhabitants use their heads instead of their hands. I recall seeing teenage schoolboys leaving afternoon school with exercise books and inkpots perched on their heads as they walk home.

One of my friends is a French doctor who, though rather wild and eccentric, has a good open mind. One evening, when we are having drinks together, in the course of the conversation I say to him: "Leblanc, what do you think about the way that these natives all carry things on their heads? Does it have any meaning as far as you can see?" He ponders for a moment and then says, "I've never given it any thought, but I cannot believe it is good for them to be made to carry great loads of bagged produce on their heads. The way you awful exploiting businessmen make them work!" I say in reply: "Well, we can't all be butchers and experiment on the poor devils, can we?" This is part of our regular exchange of badinage; all in mutual amity.

"I saw something funny the other day," he says, carrying on the gist of our conversation. "I saw a women with the usual baby strapped to her back, carrying a large tin bath full of clothes which she had been washing in the stream. She was, of course, carrying the load on her head, balanced on one of those little rings of plaited grass like they have. But suddenly this woman sees some boys playing with a football and she stops for a moment to watch them. Perhaps one of the boys is known to her - they're all related to each other as far as I can make out - but she stopped to watch them and then sat down on the ground, baby on the back and all. But she didn't take the tin bath off her head. She just sat there on the ground with this enormous bathtub of washing still balanced on her head. She didn't hold it. It was firmly balanced and she never gave it a thought."

As we laugh a little at the gestures with which he accompanies this anecdote, I say to him: "They've got to be different, apart from their skins, haven't they? I mean, how do you account for that easy balance? Neither you nor I could do it."

"They're different all right. There was a man brought into the hospital the other day who'd been knocked down by a truck in an accident. I examined him. He'd got multiple injuries of a kind that would have killed most Europeans. He was in quite a bad way and I did some immediate stitching. Within a week he was well on the way to recovery. I don't say that they can always recuperate faster or better than Europeans, but what I do think is that they can absorb physical shocks with greater resilience than we can. They've a sort of skeletal suppleness."

Soon, I start to jot down a few notes on the new subjects which have begun to interest me - pygmies, minerals, tribal differences, habits of movement and the like. There is nothing very technical about it - just a few notes for my own records.

As the war progresses, I am feeling more and more that I want to do something myself. The idea of joining the forces at this late stage, and after having gone through three years of the war as a supplies man, does not appeal. I could have become a soldier at the outbreak had not the Ministry decided to send me back to Africa. I would like to try and find some minerals myself, but I cannot do that and retain my job as Manager of the company. I have full-time obligations and loyalties to them. In the end, I realise that to get out into the bush and search for minerals is something that I really want to do. All that vast expanse of Africa is crying out to be explored and visited and I have already seen enough to want to see more.

I get in touch with Harry, the boss in Douala, who is a friend and most valued colleague. We talk it over. He says, "This venture is really not for you. You are not an experienced bush type and you are giving up a job in which you've already made quite a mark for yourself. My advice to you is to go home to England, take some leave and, if you really feel you want to do it, resign and come back. You've already done a full tour and are not in very good shape. Don't be foolhardy and be drawn into schemes of mineral prospecting for which you are neither qualified nor in a fit state of health to tackle."

I ponder this advice, given by a man whom I know to be sound. But, says a little voice inside me, if you go home to England now the war will soon end and you may never come back. You have other possibilities in England and, although you have had eight years in the Cameroons, you've not really seen the country in its far interior. If you go off on your own and look for minerals you will have accepted a challenge and - who knows - if you find them, you could perhaps make more money for yourself than your present salary? But at least you will have come face to face with real Africa.

I listen to this voice. It speaks to a hidden hunger within me. I long to go on safari with a troupe of native porters. I long to spend nights out in the open savannah and I long to do something more exciting than sending trade reports home to Liverpool. I am still only 30 years old, unmarried and waiting to be tested. There is the element of recklessness, which to a small degree is already exemplified by being a solitary Englishman in a remote French colonial town which needs to be staked and diced with. And so I negate all the sound advice and set off on a new career searching for minerals.

Of course, I have something to go on. Already, two specimens of tantalite, or what has been identified as something similar, have been handed in to the mines department. They originate in an area some 80 kilometres from a main road, in the east of the country.

CHAPTER 7

There is a Frenchman who is already a gold producer in the Betare area and he seeks me out. The word has got around that I am interested in going off into the interior to look for minerals and one day he comes into the office.

"I have been talking with the Director of Mines," he says, "and it is to him that I owe the idea of talking to you about tantalite. As you know, I already have a gold mine myself, which is not an impossible distance away from the area where the tantalite is said to occur and I would like to get involved. The price per tonne seems to be very high. If one can find it, I would be able to contribute a lot of the material needed for a prospection or even a small production. I have a spare Landrover, which is an essential, and of course I have all the other tools like prospecting pans, shovels, tents, compass, laboratory scales, density flasks and so forth. I also have some spare money for a venture."

This is almost too good to be true. I have ambitions to go into the wilds, but have no base camp, no equipment, no experience and only a limited supply of money.

"I am giving up a lot to go into a scheme to find minerals," I say. "I have a good safe pensionable job, a nice house, paid leave in England, free first-class passage to and from Africa. I don't want to be foolish and throw it all away." This is just playing the negotiating game. In my mind, I have now made up my mind to have a try and, if it fails, go home to England. If it succeeds, I plan a short leave in South Africa perhaps, before coming back and running the mining enterprise. Africa breeds resourcefulness in those who love her. Although I have no experience of mining, I have seen enough of the way that streams producing alluvial rutile are operated to I know that it only needs work, supervision and luck.

It takes me another six weeks or so to arrange for my resignation from the company, to quit my nice bungalow and prepare to abandon my comfortable standard of living. I set up a joint partnership with the gold-miner. I have been able to purchase books on prospecting, both in English and French, and to have a few books on minerals and mineralogy sent out from England. These I devour, for nothing creates a better appetite for a subject than a committed interest. And so at last I again set off to the east, but this time to the savannah country, where the native villages are fascinating, attractive little clusters of round houses with thatched roofs. Soon one sees cattle - for no cattle are permanently grazed in Yaounde - and the sight of a picturesque people who live in a state which is idyllic but one of poverty by Western criteria. Life in this part of the territory highlights the contrast between the Yaounde natives who live a town life and these country folk.

I have kept my personal house-boy and around noon we are driving off the road, as far as is practicable, across the savannah country. It is hotter than I expected, but after a few hours of driving we come to the area where the rocks begin to change. Although I am quite untutored, it is obvious that the mineral formation of these rock outcrops is different from those we have seen on the way in. There are large bands of white mineral, which I soon learn to know as feldspars. And then the rocks change again, so that they are studded with crystalline mineral. We set up camp near a stream with a deep pool of clear water and I take my first bathe in the wild. Vincent erects the tent, with the help of the driver and another boy whose services we have engaged, and soon the smell of dinner being cooked over a brush fire makes for the end of an adventurous day.

Next morning, I wake early and after breakfast begin to reconnoître the area where I must begin work. It is a marvellous place, remote with high grass waving gently in the early wind and the valleys, set out like a tapestry, rolling endlessly away. The streams are each bordered by mixed vegetation of trees, shrubs and tall grasses, which look as though a giant has embroidered them on to this vast panorama. It is majestic, a truly African view, dropping away from my elevated camp site at the source of the biggest stream.

Today, by arrangement, my gold-miner partner is due to arrive in a Landrover bringing supplies of food, drinks, tools and pans. And only an hour or two later than we have agreed, he comes over the hill to join me, smiling broadly at the former desk-bound executive, now on his own in the bush. We talk of the work that lies ahead. Of course, he has had a lot of experience prospecting for gold, but I gather that my work will not be very dissimilar to his. He has brought with him four more native porters who will do the digging and carrying and set up camps where we need. At first, however, it is agreed that we will make this place where we have first stopped the base camp, so that when we next meet, even if I am off somewhere at work, he will know that he has only to wait until I return.

Together we go down the stream and talk to each other about places to begin digging the first pits. "If I were doing this," he says, "I would make a square pit about one metre wide, one metre long and as deep as the bedrock indicates."

"Why don't we try a hole and sample this ground where we are standing?" I ask.

"Oh, no, I wouldn't advise you to do that," he says tolerantly. "You see, the mineral is leached out of the rocks and carried downstream when the rainwater flows in a torrent. That means that we have to go downstream some way and look for any signs in places where the bed is exposed."

I see the good sense of that advice.

Soon, we see places where the stream has widened and thrown up raised levels of gravelly material. We choose one of these places and set the men to dig the first hole.

"Do you know how to pan for minerals, at all?" I am asked. I admit to more ignorance.

"First you set the pan at a slight angle and begin to wash gently with a sluicing motion. You pick off the sterile lump until you gradually get down to a small residue of sand. That will contain the heavier mineral, if there is any."

"Do you often find gold when you are panning your gold prospect?" I say to him.

"You don't find it as often as I would like. Sometimes, there is only the faintest trace, but of course stream gold is pretty noticeable as it shines out against the sterile stuff."

"Well, if you are looking for black mineral, may I draw your attention to the fact that, whilst you have been teaching me how to use the pans, you have come to a nice concentration of black minerals yourself on the bottom."

Alas, black minerals abound, but they are not necessarily the ones we are seeking. My partner, who is a man well over fifty, is knowledgeable but he cannot tell tantalite from any other mineral.

Neither can I, but from my new-found knowledge skimmed off the pages of the textbooks, I know it to have a high density and should have a black/brown streak when scratched on the colour plate I have acquired. Some of the pieces we pick up in the first few prospecting pans, after slow and painstaking sluicing, are as big as my thumb nail and these I segregate carefully for testing when we return to camp. We go on for a few hours, putting down test holes, recording the dig on graphed paper, showing the position of every hole and its exact location in the stream. Generally, I collect about a dozen samples in a full day's work and then plan to work on them after I return to the camp for the evening.

Soon, I have established a routine. I set off early in the morning, shortly after daybreak, so that we can all work before the sun heats up. I choose the places where we shall put the pits down during the day, usually some 20 metres apart from each other. I take a peeled stick and make a cleft in one end for holding an identification paper, which records the number of the hole. I then set the men to dig, two to a hole, and move off to reconnoître. One thing is plain: there are over 20 streams in the immediate vicinity, each not less than a mile long, and to work them all, digging holes every 20 metres, will take much longer than I wish to spend. For I first have to find out whether there is tantalite or something else in the specimens I bring back to the camp at the end of the day. The densities seem variable. It is true I am using primitive methods to test for the specific gravity: a simple gold balance, a graduated measuring tube. I dry the material in the sun each day before weighing, but the density findings I am getting wander all over the place. From my scant information, I know that the mineral should be heavier than anything else I am likely to find, unless it's gold or cassiterite. But after a month's work, whilst I am confident that I have some heavy mineral and some not so heavy, the appearance of the mineral - whether denser or lighter - doesn't change.

Clearly, the time has come for some professional mineralogist to undertake identification, but I know that the Mines Department in Yaounde will not be able to assist. They are short staffed and under-equipped. Dr Bascombe has given me addresses to send samples for expert testing and these I prepare, one half going to Foote Mineral Co. in Chicago and the other half going to the Imperial Geological Museum in London. For a few weeks, I take the opportunity to make an overall map of the area and prepare a more permanent base camp, tentatively exploring the huge plain which stretches to the far-distant river. On the map, the major watercourse in the vicinity is shown with a stippled line, meaning that it is uncharted and unexplored.

CHAPTER 8

As each day passes, I become more and more familiar with the experience of living in the bush. At night, we always build a fire, as we have several times heard lions roaring from one of the small hills opposite our camp. Somehow, we feel no fear. We have a gun, essential for filling the pot, but it would be inadequate if ever we had to use it in self-defence. The only scare we have had was one morning, whilst walking in single file through the tall elephant grass, we heard an express train. Nearer and nearer it drew, making a rush of noise growing increasingly loud. The boys all stood still, petrified, and put a finger on their lips in a gesture telling me to be quiet and still. Soon the express train rushed past us, on into the receding distance and the stream. The boys all laughed with relief and amusement, for it was a full-grown warthog, the most dangerous animal in Africa: harmless if it does not see you, but equipped with razor sharp tusks and immense strength if moved to anger. They tell me it is short-sighted, which perhaps is as well, since it passed within 10 metres of our party.

I use the time to go on digging and prospecting. Building up a picture of the reserves of whatever mineral we have found. We know that someone identified tantalite from the area, but we are uncertain of the soundness of the test work. No one has tried to find the quantities likely to be exposed in any possible alluvial workings, and so my labours are a combination of practical daily routine and casting of bread upon the waters. But it is an exhilarating time for me. I am learning to live in the wilds and, although the rough work is being done by the boys, I share every discomfort and hardship with them. At night, I read my mineral books and even write a poem or two to send to my friend fighting in the desert army in Libya.

The days are hot and dry, but we do our work in the shade of the trees bordering the streams. There are a few flies but no malaria, so we can sleep untroubled, although regular habits, learned over the years in the west of the country, impel me to have a mosquito net each night over the camp-bed. Every morning, I give two cartridges and the gun to the hunter, an employee of my gold-miner partner. If he does not come back with something, there is trouble. I do not usually have time, except on Sunday, to go off into the higher ground where partridge and antelope abound, but one day I decide to go with him. We wander together through country dotted about with small bushes and orchard-like trees. After we have stopped to have a sandwich lunch washed down with cool stream water, a native, clothed in a loin cloth, with a sash for his bow and arrow and carrying a spear, walks by and stops to greet us. No language that I can manage is of any use, but my hunter comes from the general area and is able to exchange a few words with the visitor. In reality, it is we who are the visitors, for I learn that this man is a true hunter/gatherer, wandering the vast plains and hills of this savannah, owning allegiance to no one.

I ask him what he would do if he were injured or fell sick. He replies with a shrug of his shoulders and a smile. I sense he is a truly free man, living year after year in the wonderful, cruel, wild and open Africa which demands perfect adaptive ability as the price of survival. Secretly, I admire his courage and the inbuilt self-reliance he modestly hides. He is a braver, better, less inhibited man than I. And yet I too, in a minor way, am living in his pattern for a time, but for an end whose intention is eventually to create an enterprise to make minerals and money. He has the sun and the moon and the wind and the rain to govern his freedom. I am bound up in a destiny which is geared to a hopefully profitable mining enterprise and inevitable return trips back to England.

After a few weeks have gone by, a message is brought to me by my French gold-miner partner, who also brings luxuries such as fresh bread, butter in a cooling can, whisky, tinned meats, eggs, kerosene and toilet paper. In truth I am only a temporarily adopted son of Africa, for these gifts spell out another message to me - that after only a few weeks of isolation I am beginning to hunger for European society and its comforts. The first message is in English and is a cable from the UK, saying that the material has been provisionally identified as ilmeno-rutile and not tantalite, but that I am to persevere and if possible get together a tonne for shipment home for larger-scale evaluation. There is nothing in my books of reference about ilmeno-rutile. I know that ilmenite is a common mineral, abundant in the earth's crust. Rutile, I used to buy and have already shipped to England when I was the Manager of the company. And I have seen the way it is recovered from the stream beds. But does ilmeno-rutile mean a mineral that incorporates both? And what intrinsic value can that have? Since there is a demand for even so small a quantity as one tonne, this indicates to us that the mineral we have sampled is of some value, although we do not know what it can be. My partner and I talk things over.

"Emile," I say, "even if this is of value, it is not likely to be as valuable as tantalite and I have no idea yet how much there is in this mineral working. Some of the streams seem pretty loaded, others have the smallest possible traces in the pans, and some are sterile."

"Well, you have done well here, I reckon," he says, "and we need to get this tonne home."

"There is no way I can produce a tonne of material from an ounce or so in every pan that we wash."

He sees the sense of this at once.

"Have you been able to locate any rocks or pegmatites which contain this mineral in any quantity?" he asks me.

"No, so far I haven't, but that does not mean that there are no rocks which contain ilmeno-rutile. Do you think this could be an operation which would best be tackled from the examination of the pegmatites that are still intact, rather than working the streams where the pegmatites have been leached away?"

"Well, on the gold mine, we work both alluvial gold and the

gold-bearing quartz rock. We don't find much in the rock, but we never know when the next lodes may show. Perhaps it's the same here."

We agree that I will spend the next week or two selecting samples from the granites and pegmatites. It is far from easy, for the granites are huge monolithic features, sometimes as big as houses, and to sample these with a small geological hammer is a daunting and tedious job.

I map out the area of the rocks and begin a systematic sampling. There are no outcrops at the heads of the streams which demand attention in the way they would if filled with economic minerals. My enthusiasm begins to wane and, for the first time, I look with a tinge of regret at the folly of my venture. Have I given up a good career, local social standing, even a pension one day, in order to spend my days chipping away at a few near-sterile chunks of hard rock in an African wilderness? Other days, I am more hopeful. I am doing a wartime job, which is worthwhile, even for a tonne or two.

Occasionally, I come across a nice mineral specimen of high density ore which I mark with a red ring on the chart of the prospect area. Not having access to a laboratory is a considerable handicap, but the important thing at present is to evaluate how much visible ore there might be around. There are millions of tonnes of granite and I need only a few tonnes of ilmeno-rutile to make me feel better about the whole venture. Days pass; long, hot, discouraging days.

At the end of another six weeks' work, I have gathered hundreds of rock samples, perhaps 50 kilogrammes of stream ore, and have reached a point where it is wiser to take stock of the material won. If it is good, I can renew the search. If it is... But better not to allow those thoughts to sink roots.

My partner comes again and we agree that, until we have an evaluation, of necessity to be carried out at the Imperial Museum in London, we can do nothing other than wait. I go back again to Yaounde, this time to put up in a hotel. The man who has taken my job is a comparative stranger and provides less than the minimum hospitality that tradition requires. I am made to feel on the outside. In the space of a few months, I have lost status. Dinner tables that were open to me as a matter of routine are no longer available. I have become a prospector, associated with a gold-miner from the bush. I can bear the loss of face and income for a while, for I have been frugal during my years in the Company and have saved some money.

I decide to sit it out and let the period of waiting be a means of sorting true friends from false. But I find that kicking my heels in a second-rate hotel - for there are no good hotels in the whole country - is an abrasion of the spirit as well as a profitless drain on the pocket.

At last, the report comes from England. Again, the tests show great variety of yield. Some of the samples are worthless, some quite good. Nothing is astounding and we are as far away as ever from getting the first tonne. In fact, doing my sums, I find that there is not much return to be got simply, unless some process exists which can recover lean values of paying mineral from vast tonnages of host rock. Little as I know about the subject, I realise that a larger-scale plant would be a most difficult project, which would need much more evaluation than I could give it. And there is no proof that there are any important reserves. "Let us both go back to the mineral prospect," I say to my French partner, "and look at the whole thing afresh."

"What good will that do?" he says. "You've been looking at the place for weeks on end and have found little enough to give us encouragement. I am in favour of dropping the venture. Why don't we go off together somewhere and take a break?"

"Well, if I leave this country now, I suppose I shall go back to England. But I would also have to get a sea-passage and that may not be easy."

"The war is nearly over," he reflects, "and the best trip we could make at the present time would be to go together on holiday to South Africa. I could do with being a bachelor for a bit."

It is tempting to take up his offer. I have been working hard in a tropical country for over two years without a break and he has been in Africa, without leave, for much longer than that. Sometimes, in the Company job, we have worked all week through, from Monday morning at 6.30 until 2.30 on Sunday afternoon. After a time, the climate is enervating. Some of the French, who would normally have gone on leave to France when the war broke out, have been in the country five or six years without a change of climate. Some of them are showing the effects, both physically and spiritually. South Africa has much less appeal for them than for me as they have a language difficulty and a hunger for France which, as the war nears its end, they do not wish to dissipate on holidays outside France. To a Frenchman, Capetown is not Cannes; Durban is not Deauville.

"You're a lucky devil," says my partner. "I'd love to go home to Europe, even though I can't get to France until the war ends. But I know they won't let me go to England. I've no reason strong enough to get a wartime entry permit. But I do need a change."

"You've got your gold mine at the back of you, though," I say to him, "and that gives you a damn good income, job continuity and some long-term security. If we abandon this mineral venture, I have lost a career, money and a decent place to live, whilst I sit it out and wait for what comes next."

"Well, you can always stay at the gold mine. You know that. It is better than hanging about in Yaounde at a loose end. Shall we take a ride over to the gold mine and stay there for a few weeks?"

Prudence tells me this is the best thing to do, but if I go I remove myself from contact with the old connections - the Consul-General, friends and my old boss. I decide to go to Kribi and spend some time in the beach bungalow, which the Company owns there.

In many ways Kribi is a travel agent's dream: unspoiled, good sands, an ocean fine for swimming, surf, brochure-quality coconut palms waving their slender fronds above the roar of the surf, peaceful, idyllic. A freshwater river cascades directly into the sea over a waterfall, buttressed by rocks rising only a few yards from the edge of the ocean. There are fish to catch and eat. It seems a good spot to ponder one's present impasse and the prospects of the future.

But, as with so many tropical seaside places, there are mosquitoes, sand flies and a steamy heat. I also contract athlete's foot, which is the most serious and injurious factor. In a rundown state of health, I find that the condition soon becomes acute, so much so that I can scarcely walk. It soon becomes plain that I am badly over-tired, rather low-spirited and uncertain about my future. Furthermore, personal reasons drive me to decide to try to get back to England.

CHAPTER 9

Using some remaining influence, I secure a passage on a boat going back to England. With the addition of some 'I told you so's', and good wishes from old friends, I say farewell to my gold-miner partner and his family, and go aboard the SS Silver Laurel.

"Pride of the line, she is," says the Captain, as he comes to my cabin to visit me and see if I need anything.

"Latest high-pressure steam turbines. She's new, or almost - a nice ship to go home in."

Gradually, through the ship's grapevine we learn that our sailing instructions are to make the fastest journey we can to Freetown and join a convoy assembling there. It is December 1944.

The athlete's foot by this time is not giving concern to me alone - it is starting to smell all over the ship. I spend days in my bunk, with the cabin porthole open, my two feet protruding from the port in order to give them the benefit of fresh air and sunshine. It makes no difference. The smell gets worse.

"I'm going to put you ashore at Dakar," says the Captain. "We don't know how serious your condition is and I want you to get to a hospital as soon as possible. There is no medical care for you on the ship and I think you need it."

As soon as we reach Dakar, the ship drops anchor off the port and waits for the visit of the medical officer or a doctor. They are of course Vichy French and anti-British and resentful of the fuss made over a single British colonial being repatriated. Hundreds of Frenchmen have been in Senegal since the outbreak of war five years earlier and many have not been able to get back to France despite illnesses and medical conditions much worse than athlete's foot. The surgeon doctor takes a look at the soles of the feet, where flesh has begun to drop away, as though rotting from leprosy or gangrene.

He takes a scalpel and in two swift strokes slices down the

soles of the feet from top to bottom. It has split them open. I don't feel a thing. Pus exudes and it looks messy. But athlete's foot is not gangrene or leprosy. Given some sulpha powder twice a day on the affected area, it will clear up, says the doctor.

Three hours later, we are on our way towards Freetown. But the delay has meant that we have been left out of the convoy. Either we have to wait for the next assembly of ships to be formed, which could take a week or more, or we take a chance on sailing alone.

Eventually, we are assessed as being fast enough to steam without escort since, at the end of 1944, the submarine dangers are deemed less, obviously, than they were in those earlier journeys during the war. We sail off, the days gradually becoming cooler, the seas becoming rougher and the apprehension of being without armed protection - other than a Bofors gun on the poop - becoming greater. Ships are still being sunk, even though the Allied forces have already struck into Germany itself. The enemy hasn't given up.

At last, the coast of England appears and we shall be calling in at Falmouth for further grouping orders. At least we've made it this far. But the immigration officer at Falmouth has had a good lunch and needs a nap .

"How many are there to land?" he asks.

"Eight or nine civilians."

"Well they can't land here. They will have to go on with the crew of the ship to Hull and discharge there. They should be home before Christmas."

It takes very little time for us to build up a sense of hatred towards that callous officer. It would have meant nothing to him to clear us through customs and immigration and let us proceed at once on the long journey homeward to our families. We are merely passengers; the crew is vital to the ship's functions.

At 5.30pm, having already seen that it is very cold in England

and there is snow is on the ground, I decide to take a shower. I leave the porthole open, for although my feet are getting healthier they still have a detectable putrid smell. No sooner have I stripped for my intended hot shower, than a tremendous explosion rocks the ship. She is a big vessel of some 9,000 tonnes, but she rocks violently for a moment. The first thought is that we have struck a mine. Sea water pours through the porthole.

Boat drill has everyone familiar with our stations. I grab a blanket from the bunk and walk down the passage and climb the ladders to the deck where our lifeboat is stationed. Already, some of the crew are unhitching the boats, without hurry or haste. Some of them have been in previous attacks and survived and we all assume that if it is a mine that has caused our damage, there won't be another one.

"Get a move on, everybody," hails the Captain. "Down to the lifeboat decks, quickly please."

We have clambered down the side of the ship into the heaving boat and are just beginning to pull away. I hope nothing more is going to happen as I am perishingly cold, rather ill and have only a blanket and no lifebelt! In my illness, the regulation issue lifebelt has been overlooked. Someone has forgotten to provide one for me. Moments later, a second tremendous explosion tears the evening sky and rocks the ship. She takes it like a heavyweight boxer receiving a knockout blow. She gives a heave, groans, turns slowly on her side and then, with a rushing sound, gathering momentum she slides down into the ice-cold grey sea. Her high pressure boilers have helped to blow her midship apart. In a few moments, she is gone.

CHAPTER 10

It is now five years on. I am in my early thirties and, as might be anticipated, much has happened in the interval. I have married, fathered a daughter and become a director of a London company. I have kept up my contacts with the Cameroons, but have fallen ill again.

In fact, I am now lying in a sanatorium in Surrey, having succumbed to pulmonary TB. I have been here for eight months, lying still in bed in a ward full of other men with the same disease. It seems a rather hopeless business, for there are no drugs which can effectively handle the condition, and medical attention is based upon trying to get the body to overcome the ravages of wastage. Each day is much like the one preceding, except for visitors' afternoons which are organised on a twice-weekly basis. Food is as varied as can be expected in a well-established institution. The routine is unchanging.

The guiding principle of dealing with the illness is to ensure that patients receive plenty of rest, warmth, good food and peace and quiet. The clatter of most hospitals - kitchen noises, unthink-ingly talkative nursing staff and the like - is minimised here. But mainly it is all to little avail. This is an incurable disease, a notifiable disease, a contagious disease, a disease thought to be promoted by poor housing, poor food, lack of sanitation and poverty.

None of these conditions could have applied to me. I have lived in some luxury and ease since I came back to live in England. I have married a wonderful, loving, supportive and intelligent wife. But I suppose that the accumulation of being run-down in the tropics, with the added stress of the shipwreck, have taken their toll. And so here I am, given to bedsores and becoming increasingly fat around the waist due to lack of exercise supplemented by over-large helpings of starchy food, but not improving. The condition is remorseless.

"I am not going to be beaten by it all," says a man in the bed opposite . He has been here for 15 months, gradually becoming worse. He has followed every instruction to lie still, eat well, has taken laxatives, swallowed potions, drunk fortifiers. He has an iron will to overcome his illness. He is cheerful, determined and, despite all, happy. This is the incongruous element of the disease - it seems frequently to engender euphoria whereby dying people here are unmindful of approaching death. They have no pain and experience only slight discomforts. One expects death to come with pain. If one has no pain, how can death be very near? And yet, in the sleeping time of the night, people lie awake and fearfully grapple with the reality of their condition. They are incurables. Millions have died in and out of TB sanitoria over the past few hundred years and nothing has really changed in medicine to alter the prospects - except clinical interventions or major surgery. Better to try to go to sleep than ponder over them.

"The screens have gone round Charlie, today," says the little Irishman who is sufficiently well to be the ward's mobile gossip and newspaper supplier. A gloom settles over us. Charlie is the brave determined one. He has had some surgery, but apart from delaying the final onset of phthisis, it has done little except keep him alive in a bed. In the night, Charlie has had a major haemorrhage, whilst we were all asleep. The nurse came to him and called the matron, who called the doctor. They all look pitying and yet composed and withdrawn. It happens all the time. They see manly-looking fellows enter the wards, spend a year, sometimes two years in bed. Some, like Charlie, have become personalities, funny, cheerful, pungently cockney, leaders of badinage, ragging the young Irish nurses who seem to gravitate to this kind of hospital. And yet these fine-looking fellows end their days as thin, emaciated creatures drowning their lungs in a sea of blood which spills over on to the sheets and pillows, like the scarlet cape of a matador flung down before the dying bull.

"The screens are around Charlie." It is the euphemism for approaching death, for none of us watches another die. We do so privately, alone, but in public. Sometimes a relative sits silently beside the bed, watching the man ending his days. Wife? Father? Son? Fiancée?... It makes no difference except to those who were near and dear.

"Poor fellow," says the doctor and tells Matron to send for the next of kin. It is not Charlie's mother who will come, however. For several years, Charlie has been engaged to Griselda, who has known for long enough that she would never be able to marry him. Regular as a church clock, she has come twice a week to sit with Charlie, bringing him flowers, sweets, Lucozade.

We in the ward read our newspapers, do our writing, daydream. Charlie is wheeled away by the porters in a shrouded trolley. Goodbye Charlie.

"It makes you think," says one of the patients. Charlie was the one who would never give in, who was brave and a model. It does indeed make one think. I am on the seniority side of the inpatients now, having been in sanatoria for eight months.

Charlie's death makes me resolve to have an outside opinion. I've got to know exactly where I stand. Not very long ago, my wife brought my baby daughter to the outside window of the ward and, through the autumn afternoon, I watched my little daughter, for the first time. She was not allowed inside the building, for fear of infection. Her presence brought home to me what a burden I had become to my family, to my co-directors in the firm and to the future of a girl who may never know her father when she grows old enough to realise.

CHAPTER 11

Sir Thomas is a nice man, humane, at the top of his profession. A thoracic surgeon, he performs those dreadful operations which cut a man's ribs away to remove the irremediably diseased portions of the lungs. He looks at my X-rays. Quietly and with a warm, man-to-man look in his eyes, he tells me that I have multiple cavitation of both lungs. In the ordinary way, no doubt, patients who consult him are advised to go away and, when they are recovered enough in one lung, he will consider performing the operation. In my case and because I am insistent to know where I stand - for treating with the company about my shares, I tell him - he says straight out that I am inoperable. In the resentment I feel about the possibility of having my ribcage removed, which will make me a permanent invalid, I am glad. On the basis of the conversation, I gather it is best to prepare myself as a gentleman.

On the next visitors' day, my wife and I discuss the diagnosis. She is brave and loving and full of compassion. She has read into my letter all that needed to be said, but we are both wishing that something more could be done. There is no future in lying in a sanatorium which cannot do better than isolate and nurse whilst the body is increasingly invaded and damaged. She has got hold of a booklet advocating a diet of bacalorum, the name of some weird African plant said to have curative properties for TB. We will clutch at any straw. But she has also talked things over with her gynaecological friend, Dorothy Morrison.

It appears that Dorothy is a remarkable lady. She is a neighbour - we share the same household help - although I have never met her. But she delivered my baby daughter and has been a source of strength and encouragement to my wife during the long, drawn-out period of my illness.

"Dorothy says you ought to get out of here. We have a large house and a private garden. I can nurse you as well as or better than what you get here."

"Yes, but I have a notifiable disease; I cannot bring that into my home for you and the baby to be at risk."

"I have been at risk all the time since you came back from Africa," she says. "Sister told me right at the beginning that you've had this condition a long time. That is why you were always run-down and in poor health, getting thinner and fatigued so easily. And you are not infectious at present. I agree that you may have to go back into supervised care when infection returns, but until then..."

"I must say that I would like to get away from here. My colleagues in the company have suggested that they send me to Switzerland. The climate and diet is bound to be better than in England. But what can they do medically for me?" No answer.

"Dorothy also has another reason for wanting you to come home. She is thinking of giving up full-time local doctoring herself and is full of praises for a man called Alexander. She is a pupil of his and she wants you to go to see him."

"What is his speciality? Is he a diet man or a physician?" I ask.

"I don't understand it, I think it is something about posture or habits, but Dorothy is convinced he does wonders. Anyway, its worth giving him a chance, isn't it?"

We talk things over with the local medical officer, himself a TB sufferer, soon to die. He thinks it is a good idea for me to have a change, to go to Switzerland if I can make it. I have to conform to some regulations. He's never heard of Alexander and gives no credence at all to bacalorum.

And so, on a cold winter's day in November, I discharge myself from the sanatorium and go home. A wonderful reception awaits me as the men carry me up the stairs to a little room with a cheerful coal fire burning brightly. This will be my bedroom. By the bedside, there is a small table with a bedside light and a bowl of anemones. I face the south sun overlooking the garden.

Home diet is a stimulating change, too. Sherry in beaten egg each morning. Little dishes as appetising as can be imagined. Each day I peep around the corner of the bathroom and see my daughter, now learning to stand up in her cot and crowing "Daddy", whenever she catches a glimpse of me.

November becomes December. Alexander is not at all easy to meet. There is a long queue of people with every condition under the sun trying to get his attention. Dorothy, however, is a practising doctor who is now one of his pupils and wangles the earliest appointment she can for me to see him. He is apparently above seeking support from the medical profession, but it can do him no harm to have qualified doctors giving up their careers to learn his technique.

CHAPTER 12

The day comes when I am to go up to London to meet Alexander. I am carried down the stairs - it is the first time that I have left the floor where the bedroom is since returning from the sanatorium - and am put into the ambulance.

Alexander has a suite behind Victoria Street in London. Carried up the stairs of his consulting-rooms, I am shown into a sitting-room tastefully furnished with a few antique chairs and an elegant desk. In a few moments, Alexander enters the room, walking briskly and businesslike. He is an old man, but there is something about him that belies his age. It is more than sprightliness; he has a presence and it hides behind a young, high-pitched voice. I decide to call him 'Sir', which clearly goes down well.

"Why you people do all these terrible things to yourselves, I really don't know," he says conversationally.

Meanwhile, he has sat me down in a high-backed, hard-seated chair and moves his large, rather ugly hands about my person. First, gently on the top of my head, then on the neck which he squeezes a little between thumb and fingers. Finally he moves his hand over my back in sweeping strokes, talking to me all the time about illnesses in general.

"What do you know about my technique?" he asks.

"I'm afraid I know nothing, Sir."

"Well, I can tell you are very ill, very ill indeed."

To myself, I think the man's a mountebank. He has come into this study which contains not a single piece of medical equipment as far as I can see. He doesn't check me with a stethoscope. He obviously knows little about my particular disease, from what I have said to him. He doesn't even wear a white coat and his replies are evasive.

As if in confirmation of my impression, he simply says at the end of half an hour's consultation: "I advise you to go home and read my books. If you think you can understand what I have written, I shall be able to take you as a pupil. Dorothy has spoken about you and you should also talk with her."

I feel as though I have struggled to make the 14-mile journey to him to little purpose. After the return home again in the ambulance, I get so tired that I feel sure I will never again be able to stand the trip. Disappointment is in my voice as I tell my wife, but she has already got hold of two of Alexander's books and gives them to me to read.

"Have you read them?" I ask her.

"Well, I've skipped through them a little, but I confess I don't understand what he is saying. He does mention that he has successfully treated TB, however."

"That's not the feeling I got," I reply. "He doesn't seem to know the first thing about the disease."

I decide to read all the books anyhow, of which there are four: *Man's Supreme Inheritance*, published in 1910; *Constructive Conscious Control of the Individual*, published in 1923; *The Use of the Self*, published in 1932; and *The Universal Constant in Living*, published in 1941. I find these books to be turgid and far from clear - almost as though the writer does not want to disclose the very thing he is writing about. Written in an unfamiliar style of language, they are truly obscure. They are not 'technical', so their obscurity does not reside in the use of scientific terminology. They are not 'medical', for there is hardly a familiar medical term in them. They are not 'philosophical'. They claim nothing but, above all - and this for me proclaims their dubious value - they do not tell the reader 'what to do'.

Nevertheless, there is a reference to a wide variety of conditions and illnesses which have shown favourable responses to the 'technique'. It is a strange collection. How could any sensible person reconcile with normal everyday knowledge and experience the grouping of such dissimilar conditions such as stiff neck, slipped disc, appendicitis and TB and believe they could all be embraced within a single 'technique' - and one so simple? It emerges that it all has something to do with changing the relationship of the head to the neck.

Why can't he say how?

Nevertheless, I apply myself to reading the books, encouraged by Dorothy, who drops in once or twice a week to talk about the goings on at Ashley Place, the centre where Alexander works.

It perhaps says something for Alexander's work that famous men such as Aldous Huxley, Bernard Shaw and Sir Stafford Cripps have sat in the same chair as I have recently vacated and been taught by 'the old man'. Would men of such calibre have had the wool pulled over their eyes quite so easily? John Dewey, the leading American philosopher of his times, thinks Alexander is one of the great men of the 20th century.

Dorothy mentions that Sir Stafford Cripps has been to Alexander for a lesson that very week . He is the current Chancellor of the Exchequer and a leading lawyer. An intellectual too. It seems that if he can spare time from the House of Commons and the Treasury to go to Ashley Place, I should at least also spare time to read the books. I have nowhere to go and nothing else to occupy my time.

CHAPTER 13

Now I am truly on my own with only these 'Victorian-style' books to read. Normally, I understand, Alexander takes his pupils sitting on a chair. I am lying down in a bed at home, so therein lies a basic difference in my point of departure. But as I read, I gain a familiarity with the underlying sense which Dorothy helps to explain. And a new figure, destined to become very important in my life, has also made a brief appearance - Walter Carrington, a teacher at Ashley Place.

"Alexander discovered that the balance of the head on the neck is a vital element in the maintenance of health. Habitually, in modern Caucasians, the muscles which form the connection between skull and neck have become tense. The result is that the head is more or less drawn down into the neck or, more accurately, the skull is drawn down on to the atlas bone. Instead of the skull standing free and clear of the atlanto-occipital joint, it is tied down by these tenser muscles. The job is to free them." Not too difficult to comprehend, but not easy to change.

"How do you change your head-neck relationship?" I ask. "What do I have to do?"

The tantalising answer is that you do nothing. You don't *do*. Doing is what you don't do. Perhaps this explains why Alexander is obscure. He has found out something which, at first, only he can see and understand.

But that cannot be true or fair. Question: What is it that I cannot do? Answer: I cannot let go of my head. I cannot let it rise clear off the atlanto-occipital joint.

"Why cannot I make this change?"

"Because your whole way of doing things - moving, carrying, sitting, standing, lying - is permanently held within this narrow field of restrictions on the skull."

"That cannot be so," I say. "I can do all manner of things

without recourse to worrying about the poise of my head on my neck."

Dear Walter. Dear Dorothy. So patient, both of you, with my opinionated refusal to believe that anything important can revolve around anything so trivial. The argument goes on. I cannot release my head to let it rise up like an untethered balloon, because the way I am prevents it. It's called my psychophysical make-up. Is that me?

Better. More technical-sounding. But what does it mean?

How can I change Me?

One goes through a process: the Alexander process. One sets one's self the psychophysical task of letting the head go up. Nothing happens. It's time anyway to go to sleep. Tomorrow, we can try again. What? Not try? Sleep comes. And for several days and evenings, I find it impossible to release the head to go 'up' despite thinking about it full-time.

The first answer comes through the books - the term is inhibition - a word loaded with psychological innuendo. It doesn't mean 'inhibition' in the psychology sense; it means saying 'no'. Saying 'no' is gradually built into all thoughts concerned with the head/neck relationship. It's the prerequisite for saying 'yes'. So slowly, through the long days, a routine is developed. To let the head go up and the neck be free, say 'no' to one's self and mean 'no'. Then direct the head to go up and the neck to be free. Free of tensions. The way of 'not doing' is a new and gradually dawning way. Extraneous thought is banished from the mind and a concentration develops which is not the fixed, narrowed tenseness of concentration in the accepted everyday sense, but is a relaxed singleness of thought. That quality of thought which comes from relieving the mind of all interference and then letting 'direction' play its part.

How boring all this sounds. In the transition from exploration in thought to explanation in words, the deep secret excitement is lost. It seems to turn into jargon or become dull and incomprehensible.

After a week or so, making a little progress, perhaps, I start to feel more active. I get out of bed to go to the toilet - an elevating change of routine from the awfulness of bedpans in the sanatorium. But I do know that I've still got those bugs inside my lungs, eating their insidious way through my breathing spaces and filtering into my blood.

'Directions' are the next step in the technique. Whilst holding one's mental breath, as it were - not interfering with the thought processes of 'no' saying and letting the skull and neck release - a parallel train of thought is started up. It is to 'direct' the head to go forward. What does 'forward' mean? What does the 'head' mean?

I ask Walter. He says; "Directing your head up doesn't mean you've got to move it. It means to set your mental sights on sending your head up towards the corner of the wall with the ceiling. It is a 45-degree angle from where you are and send the mental orders to your forehead."

Send mental projections through the area of the frontal bone, so that the head is 'sent' forward and 'up'. Does he mean the head?

What is the head anyway? It is four layers of material - the musculature which envelops the skull; the bones which make up the segments of the cranium; the tissues which envelop the brain; and the three units which together make up the brain itself. That's the head. Forget the eyes or nose or mouth - they are appendages.

If it means to send the skull muscles 'up', that makes no sense. If it means the cranial bones, that makes even less sense. Sending the head 'forward and up' has, in the last analysis, got to mean sending the brain forward and up. How can one do this? Giving orders to 'direct' so that the brain has to move forward and up means a new kind of discipline or skill. How to learn it?

I re-read Alexander. He doesn't mention the brain at all, only the head. But I begin to feel that perhaps the 'head' is really another word for the brain but less fraught with dangerous implications.

In the books, it warns absolutely against trying to 'do', i.e. trying physically to make the head go forward and up. My time is short. I have nothing to lose for I am certain to die fairly soon. I will stick as close to Alexander's rules as I can, but if I'm not getting on fast enough, I will try to 'do' it - against his advice.

CHAPTER 14

Tea was nice today: toasted buns, china tea and a warm bright fire in the bedroom. The evenings draw in fast and it is cold outside. I am coming up to a point of decision about myself - that I will try to combine the non-doing repertoire with my head/neck whilst helping it along a little with a gentle push. In the bed, lying flat with head on pillow, the spine lies in a long line from skull to sacrum. My spine has been made softer and more pliable than usual by the long months of immobilisation in the sanatorium.

Well, here we go. A gentle nudge upwards. A pause. 'Let it go' says a quiet inward voice speaking straight out of the pages of one of the books. 'No one is holding it down but yourself.'

I let it go out. I give it another little nudge. Does not feel bad. Let's try a stronger push. It's not far removed from trying to hang oneself without the use of a rope. Let's now take a real risk. The small voice says 'Don't'; the other voice becomes louder and says 'try it - you have nothing to lose.'

The neck feels as though it is being stretched. Of course, that is just what must be happening. Direct the forehead out, though at the same time. It's a juggling act of keeping several streams of thought separate yet together.

Suddenly, a pressure builds up in my head - in the brain; blood seems to rush to the face and then all delight is let loose. Electrical discharges fire like rockets on a bonfire night and fill my head. There is a great relief, a blessing, a feeling of utter well-being. They say the moment before hanging is sometimes a good feeling to have, although only those who have averted the end process can know about that.

Now I'm tired. Breathing much more slowly. Women must feel like this after parturition. I lose consciousness for a moment, rouse and wake up again and then fall into a deep sleep.

Next morning, I feel so elated, I cannot wait to snuggle down under the sheets and start the process all over again. Every morning from now on is the same - and afternoons and evenings. For hours a day, I live in the compromise between directing my head to go forward and up and giving it a little extra impetus by volition. But the results are not startling, in that I am still as weak as a kitten. I would not climb three stairs in case I haven't the strength to get back again.

'Direction', as I am being told, also means telling the back to lengthen and widen. I don't seem able to do this. I need help, but I'm not convinced about Alexander. For one thing, I am not sitting in a chair but lying flat on a bed. I am in a vortex of conflicting advice. My business colleagues send a Viennese Harley Street doctor to see me.

"Open your mouth and let me take your temperature," he says.

Great Scott, has he come all this way from W1 to play games? I've been taking my own temperature every day for months. I tell him so - to no effect.

"Now, I will take your pulse."

Perhaps the Austrian accent failed to create a bond between us, but I resent the childishness.

"If you can go to Switzerland, I think you should. Your wife will take you there. Do not fly; go by train. Have a private railway carriage if you can. Switzerland will do you good."

He has gone, taking a cheque with him.

Specialists, doctors, non-medical types like Alexander, faith healers, herbalists - they are all obviously baffled by so many of the diseases which afflict the human race. I cannot think there is a way of getting multiple cavitations - holes in the lungs - to heal. One of the ways of medicine is to try and calcify the lesions, but the medicines have little benefit. Another way is to pump air into the spaces between the lung and the pleura and so build up a pressure which restricts the freedom of the lung in respiration. It cuts down the expansion of the lungs and, in theory, gives them a more settled environment in which healing can commence. There is also a theory that oxygen intake stimulates the activity of the TB bacillus, and it is logical therefore to restrict and limit the extent to which the lungs can be expanded and filled with air or oxygen.

I have been in the sanatorium about six months when an artificial pneumo-thorax is tried on me, but in a few hours the surgeon stops all further treatment of this kind as the adhesions of the lungs are too numerous.

CHAPTER 15

Each day, I have carried on working with my limited understanding of the Alexander Technique. But I have no faith, no hope, no cause to be other than realistic about my prognosis. And so, some three months after leaving the sanatorium, I agree to go to Switzerland. I can say that in consenting I have but one idea in mind - to die away from home and not to trouble my wife with the burden and care of a bedridden invalid.

We write to our dear friends Harry and Hilda in Paris. They have a beautiful apartment in the 8ième arrondissement and willingly allow my wife and myself to break our journey through France on our way to Davos by train. Harry is my former chief and colleague in the Cameroons and has now been promoted to head the Company's operations in France.

"Harry, this is so good of you." Banal, inadequate words to screen a grateful recognition that some friendships mean much more than businessmen can often recognise.

I immediately go to bed, tired beyond belief but glad that I am seeing old friends again. I feel certain it will be the last time we shall ever spend together and therefore we speak of good times past. We spent eight years in Africa together in the Company's employ But after a night's sleep, we wake to spend the final day together. Harry is well over six feet tall and weighs around 17 stone. Being a big man gives a big frame in which to hide emotions. But we all cry and cling to each other.

"I don't want to die, Harry. I am too young and I worry about my wife's position and our baby daughter left at home."

There is nothing one can say, except that perhaps the clean dry air of Switzerland will somehow help. After all, many people with TB have benefited from Switzerland's superior climate. But everything depends on the state of the disease. If one is not too advanced, rest and good air and the body's natural resistance can work wonders, although the disease is always there throughout life.

The carriage is empty and I stretch out for the long rail journey. Goodbye to it all, this lovely Europe, I say to myself as the view through the train window unfolds woods and towns and rivers in a continuous filmstrip of adieux.

The railway to Davos winds up the mountains in the snow and bright sunshine. Although exhausted and filled with the emotional conflicts of the eventual parting with my wife, I am quite glad that I have come. For one thing, there are many other people with my illness in varying stages of advancement and from all corners of Europe.

The Davos climate is agreeable at this time of year. The snow is deep and firm, the sunshine bright and uplifting. I have a private ward, which is a relief and a privilege after the public habits of the sanatorium in Surrey. There is a private balcony too, and after breakfast I am wheeled outside, covered in thick blankets and a waterproof, and lie out in the open air. I am on the top floor and see unexpected little sights - squirrels in the fir trees in the garden and snow forming at the level of the floor below me, as I am above the point where it is made. I sit for long periods watching it precipitate little flakes like mica glitter out of the clean dry air.

After a week of settling me in, my wife comes back from the Sunday service at church to tell me she is preparing to go home again. Our daughter needs her and she has seen I am in good hands here.

"Yes, you must go, darling," I say. She looks very attractive in her fur coat, velvet hat and high boots. Throughout, she has been brave and loyal and I feel a deep sense of guilt that I have fathered a child who may soon be reduced to having only one parent. I also imagine my wife as a widow and know that she will show the same bravery as she is showing as a wife.

Before she leaves she has a word with the specialist - a famous visiting professor surgeon. He has had no papers or medical history, and she tells him all she has learned from her talks with the professionals in England during my illness.

With a heavy heart she leaves me in Switzerland and goes on the long, lonely return journey to London. Within a day or so, I have thought about my situation again and I decide that I will soon take advantage of the darkness at night and go down in the lift into the outdoors. The snow is deep and the air cold. In my low state of health I will not survive long, and it is the cleanest, quietest way of leaving the world. I have long been ready.

"We are taking you today to the clinic for a test check and X-ray," says the resident medico. "You are looking a little better you know, and we will soon know if you have improved since leaving England's fogs behind you."

After breakfast, the porter wheels me out in the chair to the lift and down we go to the clinic. I submit to the familiar routine of being weighed, having urine taken for later examination, blood samples drawn and the X-ray pictures taken. It has happened so many times over the past 12 months, but the results are looked for with fear or eagerness by most patients. Extra weight means that phthisis is delayed at worst and that there is a genuine improvement in health at best. In moments of frustration in Surrey, I used to say that the blessed medicos only cared about whether I was hot or heavy. Three days later the professor surgeon pays me a visit.

"Did you say you had large cavities as well as many small ones, and in both lungs?" he asks me.

"Yes," I answer. "But any time now you will be able to see them for yourself, for my wife has made it her first task to see that the medical records are posted to you."

"Well, I have good news for you: although you have only been here less than a month, already the cavities are well on their way to being healed. You must stay in bed, of course, but if you can stay here six months, I think you will do well."

I am overwhelmed. Less than a month in Switzerland and already showing signs of healing? It cannot possibly be due to the climate or to the privacy of the ward or to anything other than what I've done myself. I have worked hard, every day since I met Alexander, doing what I believe he is advocating.

I have made considerable progress in being able to 'direct'. Each day, as soon as breakfast has been cleared away I have got down to the job of working on myself. Sometimes I can scarcely be civil to the resident house doctor, who comes round each morning for a chat. I am too busy doing my own internal work to spare time for idle discussion with him. For I have grown in aptitude. I have got into a pattern each day of lying for hours at a stretch, gradually working my mind into attentions on the head ('going up'), back ('lengthening and widening'), and neck ('being free').

CHAPTER 16

By now I am sure that the Alexander Technique contains great insights. It is a new way of organising individually motivated therapy. No longer do I think of walking off into the snow. I have got hold of something and this gives me confidence to experiment even further. On one occasion, I push my head 'up' higher than ever before. Suddenly a thin stream of warm, sticky clear fluid runs down one nostril on to my chin. As this happens, I feel a movement of liquid flowing upward in the region of the middle of the spine. It is followed by a bathing sensation over the brain. It feels utterly peaceful. But I wonder what it is all about.

Some days the changes are rapid, but more often, gradual. Skin, especially on the face, takes on a healthier look and wrinkles round the eyes begin to smooth out. I feel muscles on the scalp make slight migrations as they alter their grip on the skull bones. Some teeth even regrow enamel. Most noticeable, however, is the altered way that the rib cage expands and contracts with breathing. Rib movements are much greater, and respiration slows to five or six breaths per minute - deep, relaxed, lung-filling inspirations which rely on atmospheric pressure. All I need to do is to 'leave it alone'. The system works by itself, if left free to behave unimpeded.

When the medical history sheets from England arrive with the X-ray pictures of my lungs from the very beginning, I receive a visit from the resident doctor. He has brought a sheet of notepaper on which is typed a message. It is to the effect that I recognise that the improvement in my condition is due to the care and good conditions which Switzerland provides.

"You don't expect me to sign this, do you?" I say to the doctor. "Why do you want it?"

He hesitates.

"Well, every so often, we get recoveries which are very good and we like to publish news of them in the magazine of the sanatorium and to make them available generally to the medical people in Davos. It helps to build up the reputation of Davos as a centre for treatment."

I have to tell this man about Alexander and his wonderful discoveries and I try to explain what I know of the technique. He is interested.

"What hospital does this Alexander work at?" he asks.

"No hospital; he is not a medical man."

His expression changes and interest drains from his face. There is a suggestion of hostility because of the disclosure - that I am in this sanatorium yet following a non-medical discipline?

I adapt myself to a new attitude. I am cheerful, willing to co-operate with their temperature-takings, blood analyses, X-rays and the like, but the treatment is a secret between Alexander's books and myself. Each morning, the routine visit by medical staff brings an enquiry: "How are you, this morning?" I answer, as do most of us: "Very well thank you."

It is all meaningless. But it's the only way of exchanging information and keeping up appearances.

Daily, I feel better. After a few weeks, I get out of bed and sit out on the verandah. Then, a few weeks later, I go out for a half-hour stroll. This is always the way that convalescent patients are gradually brought into circulation again. At the end of three months, I go out into the snowbound countryside and see the early flowers starting to spring out of the grass as the snow retreats. Soon, new warmth, green fields and a myriad crocuses are joining together in the joys of a mountain springtime. I walk silently around the town, quietly thankful.

A few more days and I know that I have to get back to England, wife and Alexander. I write to let him know that I am on the way to recovery, that I owe it all to him and that I am planning shortly to return home.

The week I decide to leave Switzerland is also a week when the Zurich Cinema is showing a film on Central African pygmies.

This is a topic which has been at the back of my mind for some time and I decide that, if I have enough strength and time, I will spend my last night in Switzerland seeing the film.

Goodbye everybody, I am going home.

"You surely do not intend to fly home," says the medico. (I must qualify for being his most difficult patient yet.)

"Oh, don't worry about that," I say. "I have done a lot of flying and know I'll be all right."

It's all extremely polite, but a little controversy flares up.

"You are being obstinate and foolishly risking your life. Your lungs are not sound enough to stand that kind of journey."

"Sorry, dear doctor, but I'm going and I leave on Wednesday. My mind is made up."

CHAPTER 17

It is strange to be alone in a city again. I book into the best hotel in Zurich and, after resting an hour, hire a taxi to the cinema. The film is quite well done, scientifically. It shows two peoples in the greatest contrast imaginable - the Watussi, giant autocrats ruling the kingdom of Ruanda, and their neighbours, a host of diminutive folk who are even tinier by contrast. The Watussi have a still way of sitting and an elegant style of turning the head, which is most engaging. But it is the pygmies I am avid to see. I want to see how they are moving.

Lying in my bed in Davos, I have thought about possible connections between some of the values in the Alexander Technique and postural ways I have observed among the natives of Central Africa. Suffice it to say, for the moment, that I am looking for further evidence of the way the pygmies use their rib cages when breathing.

The deep in-filling breaths, as I have experienced them whilst immersed in the technique, are visible from the outside as large movements of the ribs. Cats display the same characteristic when they lie still in a state of relaxation. Their ribs move gently and amply. Such is their innate elegance, I have often thought it understandable that the domestic cat was worshipped by the ancient Egyptians.

The film, quite by chance and only for a second or two, suddenly shows a pygmy relaxed, breathing deeply with those motions of the ribcage which I have come to see as significant. I almost stand up and shout 'Eureka'. I now have further evidence that Alexander's work has anthropological perspectives; a fact which is merely hinted at in the books. I leave the cinema elated, full of plans to research and read everything about pygmies I can lay my hands on. I also resolve to learn as much as I can from this man Alexander, who has come to be of such importance to me. However, despite my new found optimism, I still feel very fragile and on a knife-edge.

Losing no time, I go home for a day or two and then try to

make an appointment to see him. There is no doubt that my letter to Alexander, telling him of my recovery, has caused a stir in his organisation. Dorothy comes to the house to tell me about it and to arrange for a second visit to 'the old man' - Alexander is widely known under this soubriquet. He is by now 80 years old and is passing on his knowledge to his closest associates - of whom Walter Carrington is the principal.

Alexander receives me warmly with a smile and tells me to sit down in the chair. For many long years he has been hoping for verification from someone who has trodden the path that he pioneered. Therefore my statement that I have made a sensational recovery from advanced TB is ĺof special interest to him. Having received only one lesson directly in the technique, I have acquired the rest by reading and discussion. 'The old man' says, "Now let us see how far you have got."

I stand in front of the chair. He places his hands on my head and back and levers me into a sitting position. After a few moments, he tells me to get out of the chair using the terminology of 'no-saying' and 'directing'. I do not rise from the sitting position to be standing upright in a way that is satisfactory to him. We try again.

"No, no, no," says the old man. "You haven't understood at all what I am getting at." Apparently I have committed the unpardonable offence of pulling my head back as I changed from sitting to standing. Nevertheless, I stand my ground, with a little passion in my voice. I have lived as this man's soulmate in sanatorium, hotel, aeroplane and home. I have learned almost every word of his dry-as-dust exposition. I've risked my life in his shadow.

"I may not know how to get out of a chair to satisfy you," I answer him, "but I've learnt the essence of your technique and I would be approaching death by now had I not done so."

"You haven't learned my technique. I don't know what you've done, but you are not a proper example of my technique. Now, do you want to continue taking lessons or not? It's entirely up to you."

It is infuriating to be spoken to like this. Ten minutes ago I came to his consulting rooms, a devoted, grateful, even adulatory fan and now I am told I have not learnt my lessons at all. I eat humble pie. I need this man. I say that I want to go on with him and learn his technique since, without it, I feel I cannot face up to life properly. I have too little confidence in this transitory state of so-called recovery and feel that, at any time, I could collapse and have a reversal.

It is not long before it is made plain that I have not absorbed the technique in the way that Alexander teaches it. I find it difficult to get out of a chair without pulling my head back. It is through the acquisition of this skill that so much of the effectiveness of Alexander's work is obtained. Walter Carrington increasingly takes over the job of teaching me.

"Walter, there seem to be two kinds of teaching. The 'old man' just wants to get you out of a chair without your head being pulled back, and gives you verbal hell if you don't succeed. Today, he told me I was wasting everybody's time because I will not think. The special kind of thinking he talks about may seem easy to him but it's tricky for me. The other kind of teaching, which you go in for, is to let me spend a lot of the time stretched out on the table with a few books under my head for a pillow. That is more familiar to me, because that is how I taught myself in bed. No one can deny that I got fantastic results from working on myself in bed, but I now know that I haven't been able to perform exactly as the old man wants it. I also find him a cantankerous old devil, with a very irritating way of getting under my skin."

Walter laughs, "You have it for three half-hour sessions a week. We have it every day and all day. But the old man can do so much more with the chair technique than any of the rest of us, so you'd best put up with it."

"This business of getting out of a chair, 'by not doing'. What is it all about?"

"It's just something the old man has in his hands. That's the view of numerous medical folk who've looked into the technique."

Perhaps it is so. For although that would not make it any less wonderful to experience, at least it would put him into a category - alongside those healers whose gifts are not understood but are known to exist. The difference with the old man is that he put it there alone, untaught. No one helped him; no one gave him lessons; no one puts him on a couch to get his head out or his neck to 'undo'. He did it deliberately and alone by 'non-doing'.

What is it that the old man does when he gets someone out of a chair? He has treated thousands of people, from the most famous down to the simplest folk. There is an enigma here. One won't discover it looking into textbooks, for no one has written about the 'what'. People like Aldous Huxley have written around the subject and Alexander's work is often mentioned in his writings: *Eyeless in Gaza* and *Ends And Means* are but two of the works containing references to Alexander's ideas. Alexander himself does not explain his system in 'what it is' or 'how it works' principles, but in the main confines himself to touching upon the issue implicitly, with 'psychological' interpretations and insights. So, what does he actually do? I ask him outright and again I am castigated for the manner of putting the question.

"The technique is about non-doing. The first question you ask is to find out what it is that I do? Will you never learn?"

That shuts me up - for a short time.

'But,' says the prompter hiding inside my ear, 'if he is not doing something, it seems logical that he is doing nothing, which is plainly absurd. Are we simply hooked on odd-ball meanings of words - like the difficulty of interpreting what 'inhibit' means.'

CHAPTER 18

It is an entirely new sensation when one has a good lesson in the technique. Getting up out of a chair is to pass through a change in posture which is effected in a way contrary to the normal laws of gravity. Perhaps the way to open up the understanding is to describe first what it feels like. One is 'spirited' up. There is a secret way which is put into operation, once habitual ways are eliminated by the 'no-saying'. By directing your thoughts into channels, legs and knees are prevented from stiffening, 'release' of the head is promoted and the 'spirited way' appears. One moment you are sitting in a chair, the next moment you have slid effortlessly to a standing position.

There is a party trick we used to play when we were young. One of us would sit in a chair, the rest would pile their hands on his head and press down. At a signal, all hands would be taken off and fingers would be placed under the knees and armpits. The body had in some way acquired 'anti-gravity' force which meant that the release of the pressure on the head made the body lighter, so that it became easy to lift on the finger tips.

It was a trick which would not work on everyone, but if and when you did experience it, it made you feel 'curious uplifting' energies which are hidden away in the body. Alexander's technique is not a party trick. It is a system of re-education which uses the anti-gravity mechanism to change all the systems of the body. Until you experience it, you cannot believe it. But as I shall relate, all systems change.

Whilst I was having my lessons from Walter there was a girl who always seemed to have booked the appointment before mine. I was able to see how she changed over the period of the teaching. She grew taller, fitter-looking, more slender and altogether more healthy. She underwent a visible metamorphosis during those weeks. I never learned her name, but we used to enthuse over each other's visible improvement as the weeks went by. The implications of this are more than just simple changes of 'use', to employ Alexander's terminology. 'Use' is the way you move your head, body, legs and feet in motion. The 'old man' drew attention, before it was generally discussed, to the theory that the Caucasian race has degenerated in many physical ways. People throw their heads about in disproportionately extravagant motions. If they sit in armchairs they often twist their legs into tight knots. Even their hands are never still but are clenched in inappropriate tensions. Teeth are gritted, jaws are clamped together - there is a host of tell-tale signs that our 'use' has fallen away from the ideal which once existed.

The technique is about restoring us to that former standard of 'use' and it might seem that you have to cut your way through many disciplines. Unless he be another Goethe, no man can expect to have more than a nodding acquaintance with all the subjects which could be said to be embraced by the technique. Alexander's way was to keep it simple. In so doing he limited his own vision of his work, but he kept the vision clear and untrammelled. Physiology, anthropology, psychology, anatomy are but a few of the related areas of science which might be drawn upon in examination of the results.

It is better to attempt an understanding than adopt the attitude of the professor from Wales who, given a demonstration by Alexander, jumped out of his chair and left the room for ever, saying: "I'll have nothing to do with black magic." But something special does happen to your body when you have gone through a number of these sessions 'getting out of the chair'.

"Don't wear it out," says Walter, when I tell him I am practising the technique by the hour. Wear out what? Here we come to one of the real conundrums of the work. The old man claims in his writings that there is something called the 'primary control'. When Walter warns against 'wearing it out', he means don't overtire the primary control.

There does not appear to be any such structure, anatomically speaking. There is no single organ to which one can point and say, 'That is the part that controls and brings about the re-coordination of all the body.' And yet...

I've just boarded the underground train at Victoria and am on my way to Westminster Station - two stops, five minutes.

As I sit down in the carriage, I feel as though inside my lungs and throat there is a source of fizzing energies, a releasing effervescence which fills my mouth. The fizz feeling originates in my lungs, comes up the windpipe and starts to inflate my tongue so that it swells. It becomes a fleshy mass, which bloats and fills my mouth. It all feels very weird. A torrent of bio-electrical discharges half-chokes me as I sit in the train. By the time I get to Westminster, it has virtually passed and I have a great sense of relief. It's done me a power of good. Primary control?

A day or two later I have been 'directing' as usual - this time to let the knees relax and 'let go'. I have a feeling of coming into contact, for the first time in my life, with the inner strings which actuate the bony skeleton. The strings lose their habitual slackness and the joints of the skeleton, from feet to neck, are gradually tautened. It is most pleasurable and makes me feel more integrated. Primary control?

I notice now that I am gaining in energy. I still do not feel up to going back to work, for the prospect of resuming the pressures of business dismays me. But I become an avid reader and an early investment is in a textbook of anatomy. I've got to see what the bits of the body that interest me look like.

Let us summarise what has so far been achieved:

1. Virtual recovery from a fatal prognosis following advanced TB with healing of numerous disseminated large cavities. I have done this almost unaided, except for readings.

2. Regenerated lungs and skeleton, so that I feel healthier.

3. Grown at least an inch taller.
4. None of my suits is now big enough.
5. Hats now have to be 1/8th larger in size.
6. I've learned to sit still.
7. Memory and judgement are better.

I've still not identified what the 'primary control' might be, but I know beyond a shadow of doubt that the results of (2) to (7) inclusive have been developed through the Alexander system. By comparison with the attitude of some of his mainstream medical counterparts, Alexander's integrity of purpose shines brightly and honestly. Alexander is a truly great and exceptional man.

CHAPTER 19

Growing taller in the mid-thirties of life is an experience which is uncommon, except in the Alexander work. Plenty of people have been similarly changed. Tallness is gradually developed, as direction of the head to go 'forward and up' becomes a routine part of everyday behaviour. It is thinking in action. But the feeling of actually being pulled up by the muscles of the skull made me look a lot closer at the textbook. However one views the elusive 'primary control', it is unlikely to be just an upward pull by the suboccipital muscles, pulling towards their broader end at their attachment to the skull. That action alone would not bring about great nervous and structural modifications. So it must be due to some other part of the anatomy which is involved when the head is 'freed', enabling the suboccipital muscles to begin their gentle tractions.

This raises the question: What parts of the head/neck structure are also involved? Drawings of the head, neck and spine in the textbook show quite clearly what is implicated. When these muscles act upwards on the atlas and the spinal column, they are also involving that which lies inside the spine itself - the cord complex itself. The segment of the nervous system located at the top of the cord - principally the medulla - is placed under special influences. It is also subjected to being pulled upwards. The minute motions of the suboccipitals on the outside and the spinal cord on the inside are such as to draw up the medulla through the foramen magnum. This can happen only when the suboccipital muscles work in their 'anti-gravity' way, by releasing their grip on the atlas joint. The skull is like the lid on a steam kettle. If the kettle begins to boil, the skull acts out its capacity to rise up and fall back down again on to the atlas.

As Walter says: "Let it float off."

Alexander called the phenomenon which happens when the head goes forward and up the primary control. This is the way to start this inner work by the nervous system. This is the base from which the transformations are brought about and they are carried on primarily in changes of attitude by the medulla.

'Pulling down', in Alexander's terminology, means implicating the medulla in congestion. 'Going up' means releasing the head from its suboccipital muscle ties so that the medulla is set free. This has obvious anthropological significance in terms of human evolution.

I decide to make some visits to the British Museum, the Royal Anthropological Institute and the Horniman. I also use the libraries near to my home. In addition, I would like to make contact with people who are professionally interested in skulls, ancient and modern.

CHAPTER 20

Autumn is already here, coming after a gorgeous hot summer. Life for me has become truly delightful. I read a lot, go up to Victoria three times a week to spend an hour with Alexander or Walter and then go off to one of the museums. The very first time I visit the British Museum, I see a cabinet of head rests, collected from remote places such as Borneo and the South Seas. The only places I have hitherto seen head rests are in the hospital in Yaounde and Alexander's teaching rooms in Victoria. His are merely piles of books placed under the pupil's heads, so that adjustments can be made easily to their height. Significantly, they are hard books and the head rests in the museum are made of hardwood. What, I ask myself, is the purpose of using a hard pillow made of wood?

At home that day, I take a block of oak and cut a shallow dish out of it for my head to lie on. It is far too hard and uncomfortable. I use a pile of books, but they tend to slide about. Soon, I find out that one good thick book will do and I use this when I lie down in the garden, watching my baby daughter exploring as she crawls around. I also throw out the pillows from my bed and take to sleeping at night with the book under my head. It's hard at first, but one gets to like it, for it has a special relevance to the head/neck positions that Alexander has discovered. Who else in the world uses hard pillows and did we Caucasians ever use them?

If so, when did we cease to do so? Fortunately, there are still plenty of photographs available in magazines, such as the Geographical Society's monthly editions. The Japanese use flat bamboo pillows and lie mainly on the floor or on a hard surface. The Chinese use a lacquered and dished hard pillow. The ancient Egyptians are well represented in the museum - they used concave wooden half-yolks mounted on pillars. So many different peoples have used hard objects on which to lay their heads. Many peoples do still, but many others have abandoned the practice. Might this

The author with his wife and baby daughter

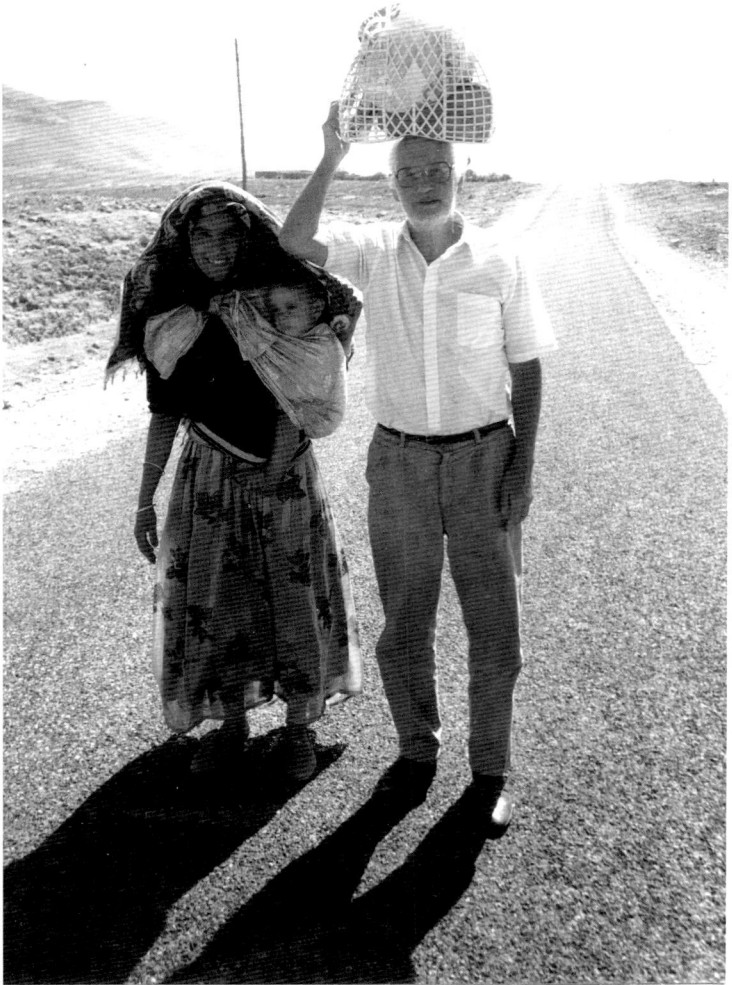

The author demonstrating head portering
in Morocco

be a line for worthwhile investigation?

I read that Norwegians used to stuff pillows with horsehair so that they became solid. I read that Italians used to fill cotton pillows tightly with pine cones. I read that, even in Britain, in the 16th century, servants at Hardwick Hall in Derbyshire are recorded as having slept on wooden headrests.

Today, in our comfortable warm beds, we sleep with one, two or even three soft downy pillows. We have changed the way we treat our head/neck relationship, presumably because it is warmer to have a downy soft pillow under the head rather than a cold hard block. Conversely, though, might it also be true that a hard pillow is used in countries where it is too hot to use a soft warming surface?

In what other directions can we investigate the changes which Europeans, for instance, have evolved in their resting habits? Beds are a fascinating subject if considered worldwide. Most of the world's populations still sleep on hard flat surfaces. It is mainly we Caucasians who have changed. We sleep on mattresses with springs instead of wooden slats or boards as the support. Soft adaptable surfaces such as are found in sprung beds are warmer again, but they are a radically different environment for the recumbent spine.

My memory switches me back to Yaounde days. Not only do the native patients in the hospital lie on hard wooden beds, but they greatly prefer them to sprung mattresses. They feel their bodies are more supported. I now also remember a French friend who had a half-caste mistress. She would begin the night in his soft bed but, after an hour or so, preferred to hop out and lie on a mat alongside the bed for the rest of the night.

Millions of people now living in the world prefer to sleep on hard surfaces, despite the advances in so-called comfort wrought by the 20th century. These peoples do not, in the main, include the white Caucasians. In the Alexander teaching centre, you are placed on a hard-topped table and made to lie flat on your back. The books are put under your head, adjusted suitably to the head-height.

Where is the parallel between the posture changes brought about by the Alexander work and the history of postures as a worldwide phenomenon?

"Walter," I ask, "what kind of bed and pillow do you use?"

He thinks the question odd. If the technique is taught on a hard-surfaced pillow and table, might it not be beneficial to persons like me to use the same principles at home? It seems impertinent to ask Alexander how he sleeps, but I find out that he just goes to rest on a bed with a firm mattress. Neither F.M. nor Walter has spent years in Central Africa, seeing how the natives do these things. I decide, somewhat to the consternation of my domestic household, to move out of my bed and start to sleep on the floor at night. I'm going to start doing some things in the ways that I have seen natives in Yaounde do them.

Lying on the hard floor at night with a sheet spread over the carpet, I soon understand why people sleep in beds in Europe. I feel cold and, at first, uncomfortable. But since everything is to be sacrificed to learning the technique, I have concluded for myself that I ought to carry the technique's methods into my own bedroom.

Undoubtedly, it helps. I find I can not only 'direct' my head out more easily, but the hard pillow (the big book) helps the process. You can't wriggle about so much. The skull soon gets used to the slight discomfort of being laid on the book and the moving off the atlas joint is assisted, subtly. Lying flat on the back all night brings about a change in the feel of the skeletal bones. Sore at first, they soon adapt, and in the final result it becomes uncomfortable to me to have to sleep in a normal hotel bed. Indeed, soon after, I have occasion to attend a short business session and a suite at the Ritz Hotel in Piccadilly has been taken for us. We talk, finish our business and then at night I go to my room and pull the clothes off the bed and lie on the floor. It says much for the aplomb of the valet next morning when he asks: "Where would you like to have your morning tea, sir?" without a trace of surprise in his voice after finding me asleep beside the bed.

Chinese, Japanese, Asiatics of all kinds, Negroes, Arabs, Indians - all these races include millions who sleep on the hard uncompromising surfaces of the beaten earth or the board floor - many from necessity, many from choice; and one feels somehow that in earlier times, perhaps less than a century ago, the peoples of the earth contained a higher proportion who consigned their bodies nightly to a hard surface for support. Bodily habits have changed. The question is where to find the evidence?

Let us look at chairs. Although there are still a few peoples who do not habitually sit on a chair, in the main the world has learned to use them. But as close to home as England, the changes in the design of the chairs of today, compared with the chairs used by the Victorians, are striking. The sitting attitude of the Victorians was quite different. I ask one of my business colleagues - who must surely be getting a little restive that I can spend time looking into these rather odd trifles but none on the business - how I can get hold of photographs of Victorians to compare them with people doing the same kind of job today.

"Why don't we take a look at one or two of the long-established boardrooms?" he says.

We make a visit to a member of the London Metal Exchange and there, plain for all to see, are upright, straight-as-a-ramrod-back kind of men in their Victorian photographs. Today's men are less upright. But I don't get pictures of chairs. For that I have to look at the salerooms and furniture shops selling Victoriana, and try sitting in such chairs myself. The contrast between the low, easy club-room deep armchairs and the hard-bottomed seating of the upright Victorian chair is astounding. Photographs indicate that crossing the legs at the knees was not common, whereas today it is difficult to find Englishmen sitting in a chair with the legs uncrossed. The most salient contrast, however, is the general impression of uprightness. The Victorians, to a man, look as though they have had lessons from Alexander, although he was not yet born when some of the photographs were taken.

At all events, it would appear that Alexander had a point when he stated that modern men - that is, men of this century - have deteriorated in posture. The photographs are there for all to see. A man who sits slumped in a low-slung armchair or settee, often manufactured with a tilted back for attractiveness of design, is placing his spine in a totally different environment from the man who sits on a hard seat with a straight-up back. In fact, it is now becoming exceptional to see people sitting truly upright in the way that a pupil at an Alexander school is taught to sit.

CHAPTER 21

I go back to the British Museum and apply for a reader's ticket. By now, I have also joined the Royal Anthropological Institute and have been able to browse in its library. My days are spent between the two. Apart from acquiring new knowledge about anthropology and the evolution of man, I am also interested in trying to identify the changes in my own body as I progress under tuition from Alexander and Walter Carrington.

The British Museum's amazing reading room makes books available which disclose the most unlikely relics of the past. I read, with great interest, of Koller's rejected theory that man, in his ascent, passed through a pygmy stage. Certainly there is no way that such a theory can be reconciled with current doctrine, for every succeeding year seems to reveal an increasingly older and totally divergent type of prehistoric skull. It truly is bewildering. The pygmy does not seem to have an accepted place in the scheme of things. No one has a theory which is acceptable to all. Even Darwin's monumental life work holds creaking conclusions which palaeontology does not sustain in an unqualified way.

Pondering these problems, I decide that the most logical way for me to proceed is to read the accounts of travellers and anthropologists who have actually been among the Central African pygmies. It is surprising how many anthropological works include judgements about the significance of pygmies by people who have no first-hand knowledge of them.

I start to make lists. What have we here? R.P. Trilles, *The Pygmies of The Equatorial Forest* (1932). I read this but find little out of the ordinary. Schweinfurth writes quite substantially, but there is nothing to astound one. P. Schebesta's *Among Congo Pygmies* (1929) is far more promising:

> My eyes took in the strange contours of his yellowish-clay coloured body. It is only amongst pygmies that one finds such a strange

conglomeration of physical abnormalities. Actually, in addition to their short stature and their queer-shaped heads, their bodily proportions or rather disproportions, form such a striking feature that you could never mistake them for specimens of any other race. The thin short legs are in direct contrast to the long thick trunk, with its square broad shoulders. Their arms were abnormally long, but their hands and feet seem almost shapely, although the latter are frequently introverted. Though his legs, arms and chest were covered with a fairly thick coat of hair, my companion's body was not nearly as hirsute as those of the other pygmies I met later. Agali was hideously ugly. I sought comfort in the hope that his fellow tribesmen might have more pleasant and attractive features. In this, I was utterly mistaken. Almost all the pygmies that I met later - and they numbered thousands - were indescribably repulsive, many so hideous that they made me shudder. The children for a few years are quite attractive, but nobody can blame the pygmies if they harbour a grudge against their creator for making them so appallingly ugly; although all primitive men in bygone ages may have looked as repellent as they. Another striking characteristic among the majority of the pygmies is their bright brown skin. There are some dark mannequins and even jet black ones. The latter, however, are very rare and are found exclusively on the outskirts of the forest, so that in all probability, they are half breeds. The bright tint of the Bambuti skin appeals so much to the Negroes that they often refer to them as their brothers. I learned later that the average height of the Bambuti male is 3 feet 8 inches and that of the women 3 feet 4 inches. I saw men, women and children swaying in a measured dance. There they were, those golden brown Congo dwarfs with their queer angular faces.

He is writing about the Bambuti, who are called Basua by the Babali Negroes, but they call themselves by many names over widely scattered areas. There are many distinct and separate groups of pygmy. Although Schebesta is writing about the average height of pygmies who are exceptionally small, the general features he outlines seem much closer than for other writers to the description of the group I saw myself that day in Yokadouma. He has found a better way of picturing their strangeness than I was able to, but it is reassuring that I am not alone in the privilege of having seen such people. Moreover, he is talking about pygmies who live a great distance away from the area in the Cameroons with which I am familiar. The Bambuti are located in the Congo.

I pick up a book by Montandon, a famous French anthropologist, writing in 1928. For me, he expresses the question perfectly. "What is the most delicate point in the problem of human phylogeny? It is certainly the question of the attachment of pygmies to the common trunk. In the end and whichever method one adopts - polygeneticism, monogenetisism - one can conceive of several ways of relating human races and hominid types, if we exclude the problem of the pygmies."

Montandon goes on to widen the framework in which the significance of pygmies can be considered generally. He correctly says that in general terms today they occupy a long Equatorial strip in the Congo, in former German East Africa, in the Andaman Islands, in the Malaccan Peninsula, in the Phillipines, in New Guinea and the New Hebrides. Their most common feature is their stature from 1.4m to 1.5m for men and 1.35m to 1.45m for women.

However, I am not very interested in pygmies other than those in the Central African belt. The Belgian Congo seems to be their main location, but other areas such as French Congo, Cameroon, Gabon, even Kenya, have all had pygmy tribes and some are still dwelling there. But the kind that interests me especially has to be very small and timid, to have light-coloured skin and be physically distinct from the more robust black- or dark-brown-skinned pygmies, who might be deemed to have come further along the evolutionary road.

I tell Alexander about my pygmy experience in Africa - the exceptional ones in Yokadouma, not the everyday sights of Akonolinga or Ebolowa pygmies which anyone could have seen. Alexander listens with interest, but says nothing. I turn again to Schebesta. "A market is held in Avakubi on certain fixed days.

Among the ranks of half-naked women, I saw some strange tiny golden brown creatures who as soon as they caught a glimpse of the white man, dived for cover."

Bless you, Reverend Father Paul Schebesta. You and I have shared the same experience in totally different parts of the Ituri Forest. At least I am not alone. I go out of the British Musem into the cool rain of a London afternoon, elated that I have found at least one other writer who gives support and credence to what I've said. The 68 bus home follows the kind of dull route through South London that encourages introspection. Staring unseeingly at the monotonous drabness of it all, I make a small resolve that one day I shall go back to the Cameroons and spend time among the pygmies. It will mean taking time away from my business, but life is now split between this overwhelming interest in evolution and the need to think of earning a living again. It is almost two years since I did a stroke of work and we shall soon need money.

The point of decision is soon to come. My wife and I talk things over. I would like to become an anthropologist, I tell her. I have no degree of any kind and am not particularly gifted at academic things. We talk over the risk of trying to establish myself in the intellectual jungle, and try to assess it in comparison with business life. It does not take me long to see that infighting and competition for ideas and status in academic circles are just as keen as anything we have in commerce. I am finally convinced when I attend one of the Royal Anthropological meetings at which Professor Le Gros Clark and Professor Solly Zuckerman argue the significance of variations in chimpanzee skulls which have originated in the Cameroons. I realise I would have no chance of making a living as a physical anthropologist. As I have a wife and daughter to think of, as well as the matter of loyalty to colleagues who have been very kind and supportive during my long illness, the decision to go back to work is not hard to make.

But there are books to read still, and I start compiling a list and extracting notes of anything significant. E. Torday, *On the Trail of the Bushgongo* (1925): I note, 'all dark skinned' - therefore of no interest to me.

J.T. Harrison, *Life Among the Pygmies of Ituri* (1905): "I do not ever remember seeing such a wonderful variety, so many types and extremes. General height from 3'10" to 4'5", (1.17m to 1.35m) black to horrible sickly yellow."

Inventaire Ethnique Du Sud Cameroun (1949):

> The existence of pygmies in the Cameroun, long the subject of discussion, is no longer in doubt. There are 3 quite unequal groups. (1) Administrative areas of Batouri - Subdiv. Yokadouma (2) Abongmbang - subdiv. Lomie - Akonolinga (3) Ebolowa (subdiv. Edea and Sangmelima) although they present a distinctly different physical appearance from the Negroes. They are less characteristic than the Ituri pygmies; they are pygmoids, rather than true pygmies.

Another day, I pick up Sir Harry Johnson, *George Grenfell and the Congo* (1908). All descriptions of these dwarf forest dwellers throughout West Central Africa unite in emphasising the following points:

> They are yellow or reddish, yellow-skinned; much short 'felted' body hair, flat broad noses and with well proportioned bodies, but with short weak necks. Adult males seldom above 4ft. (1m.20) Strong skin smell. What is further remarkable is the association of certain widespread tribal names with both pygmies and dissimilar Negroes of ordinary or tall stature.

I read something of particular interest in De Quatrefarge's book, *The Pygmies* (1895):

> The notably yellow-skinned pygmies, over a wide area, have generally been observed to be the smaller type, rarely exceeding 1.30m. The darker skinned type ranging from 1.30m to 1.50m. In a second group, with notably yellow-skins, a list can be compiled of reports of their salient characteristics as follows:-

Explorer	Area	Height (Metres)
F. De Langle	Nonspecific	0.98 average
Breschin	Congo River	0.90 very yellow?
Barrow	Sangmelima	1.14
Stanley	Ituri	1.15 - 1.30
Verner	Kasai	1.13 average
Gaillard	Sangha	1.30
Kund	Yaounde	1.23

R.P. Trilles (1932) found somewhat similar results. Light-skinned males - 1.30m to 1.35m max with women 0.905m to 1.31m max. Dark-skinned males - 1.47m up to 1.52m; smallest, 1.36m.

Sir Henry Morton Stanley met his first pygmy in the Ituri in 1887 and describes her as a perfectly formed young woman about 17 years old, who measured 33 inches (0.84m) in height. She was the colour of yellow ivory.

Another 19th-century explorer was Mounteney-Jephson, who wrote of his travels in 1880 that the pygmies he met were light-brown reddish in colour, sometimes yellowish, and were mostly 4 feet to 4 feet 1 inches high (1.22m to 1.24m). That is 6 inches (15 cms) less than the same Mbuti people average today.

I find a fascinating entry in the *Société D'Études Camerounaises* (1943), written by Maurice Bertaut, who was the *Chef De Région* at the time I passed through on my way to Yokadouma. Bertaut writes:

I've seen negrillos in the forest, but never in the Savannah, in the region of the Haut Nyong. I was able to approach 5 groups of negrillos, spread between the areas of Doumie and Djaposten. I know that negrillos also exist in the subdivision of Messamena. As one travels E-S-E, the more one meets them. In the subdivisions of Lomie, Yokadouma and Mouloundou, it seems that they are very numerous. It would be interesting to know how many. It would appear that the Cameroons' negrillos are more evolved as one travels west, (i.e. nearer to the sea coast) generally. The Babinga are either called pygmies or negrillos. I prefer to call them negrillos, reserving the name 'pygmy' to men smaller than our Babinga. I do not think I have ever met a real pygmy, free of any crossbreeding; but I have seen many Babinga. Someone who is not alert could pass by the negrillos without noticing them. However, as soon as one has really observed a few, one can no longer mistake them. But it is rather difficult to say where they differ from other blacks. Height 1.41m to 1.68m, average 1.529m.

Bertaut goes on to add that:

R.P. Trilles found many much smaller examples than I give. I doubtless found myself in the presence of negrillos who were crossed. Their skin colour is distinctive. In fact, it is recognised that the purer the strain, the lighter the skin: rosy yellow to dark grey 'pigskin'. "The individuals I saw," remarks Bertaut, "were dark skinned since they were hybrids, but looking at them closely, one could see that they were unequally coloured. They are more dirty-brown than black and women are much lighter skinned than men. They do not suffer from leprosy or sleeping sickness, which are such a flail among the sedentary natives of the region."

It should be recalled that Bertaut, as the Chief Administrative Officer, lived years in these regions and I was simply astounded to read his disclosure that he had never met a 'true' pygmy. It now makes me realise how tremendously privileged I was.

There is more reading to be done. Most authors are either German or French. I plough through all that I can trace in the library of the Royal Anthropological Institute and the British Museum. I write to the Musée de l'Homme in Paris and obtain information from there. But in the end, there is but little to be gained from further reading. I have to think the next phase out for myself. Clearly, it is not good enough to dismiss the modern pygmy as an aberrant race. It would seem essential to understand exactly where they fit in to the evolutionary pattern, for it may well be that a proper understanding would cause a major modification in the current view of man's ascent. However, this is an intellectual quest riddled with potential pitfalls. I try to identify some of the points needing an answer.

1. What has happened to the "tiny, yellow-skinned timid figures" observed by Breschin, Fleuriot De l'Angle, Schebesta and myself?
2. How is it that, as the century progresses from late 19th until the mid-20th, the many pygmies who have been measured for height, arm length, leg length, etc. appear to be so different now from those earlier times when they were first examined?
3. How do we explain the fact that the peoples who live in proximity to the forest pygmies, i.e. in the savannah lands which were once forest, are also small in stature and have skins which appear as if they have undercoats of yellowish tints?
4. What, if any, is the evolutionary relationship between pygmies and negrillos who live in the Savannah areas?
5. No matter how diligently one explores the forest today, it is virtually impossible to find the little yellow creatures glimpsed, albeit rarely, earlier in the century. Is it possible that they have metamorphosed?

Many races have changed rapidly in some of their physical characteristics as their environments have changed. The Poles who emigrated to America at the turn of the century grew six inches taller in one generation. The British themselves, as anyone will know who has been in a Tudor-period house or cottage, were small compared with our contemporaries today, and the evidence of 15th- and 16th-century skeletons confirms the change. But the changes in the pygmy peoples of Central Africa, both generally and individually, appear to be of a totally different magnitude and order.

CHAPTER 22

I resume my life as a bowler-hatted London businessman, working in Victoria Street in Westminster. Each morning I catch the 8.30 train from home in the suburb of Norwood, and return home again at 6 o'clock in the evening. It's an existence typical of millions of Londoners and so utterly different from the expansive life of a colonial living in beautiful, tropical Yaounde. I keep up my friendship with the son-in-law of the gold-miner, who still lives in the Cameroons, looking after the family's business interests. We write to each other often, and when he comes home to Paris on leave I always go over and spend a few days with him. We talk of the minerals I tried to prospect and decide to make another attempt together to develop some of the minerals known to exist in the Cameroons.

"Why don't we form a company together?" he says. "You can look after the selling and shipping of anything we find and produce, and there is always rutile. We can make a start with that."

The lump rutile of the Cameroons, dug by hand from the small streams where it occurs as an alluvial product, has yet to meet the competition from Australian beach sands, which will soon dominate the world market. In fact, although it is easy to win, the Cameroon quality is not really consistent enough to compete with the Australian product. But the world is short of rutile and we can sell ours into the small, specialist colours and glaze trade in the Potteries.

Soon the *Cie Camerounaise des Minerais* is born and it ships a few tonnes of rutile home to England. It sells quite well. I form a little mineral department in the Company to trade and if possible extend our knowledge and connections with the mineral business generally. Friends in the mines department of the Ministry in Paris keep in touch with me, and I start to interest large companies in the unknown possibilities for prospecting in the Cameroons. One of the large American groups, with a British office in London, shows interest in looking at the tantalite possibilities and I draw upon my abortive wartime experience to try to get them to support the *Cie Camerounaise* and undertake properly capitalised prospection by qualified geologists. They agree. The managing director himself decides to fly out to Africa and look at our old prospecting areas. I sit in my office in London whilst he goes out to the Cameroons and is taken to the sites. He comes back distinctly discouraged. The occurrences of the mineral are not sufficient in size to justify a large-scale operation and the Americans withdraw. But it has been a good experience for me. I have met executives of a worldwide mining company and seen how they go about their studies of African resources.

At home in Norwood I continue my Jekyll and Hyde life of being a businessman in the day and a student of anthropology in the evening. There is a little ornamental park nearby and in the summer evenings I go there as dusk approaches and begin a minor series of studies on myself, using the Alexander Technique and trying to develop more experience, at first-hand, of the postural variants which my studies have indicated.

First, I find a secluded bench, hidden behind shrubs and trees where few passers-by are likely to disturb me. I begin by getting up from sitting on the bench to a standing position in the way that Alexander teaches. I pay great attention to the head/neck relationship as I do this, and now that I have become reasonably adept, I soon begin to experience the 'anti-gravity' sensations the technique engenders.

When I feel as though my head is 'up' enough, I take off my shoes and socks and begin walking gingerly on the grass and paths in my bare feet. In this way, I learn to feel the soles of my feet as they expand under the pressures of each step. All the Africans I am familiar with - Negroes, negrillos, pygmies - walk barefoot for preference. Some even play football to a high standard wearing no boots, and manage to effect prodigious kicks of the ball with their bare toes.

It is not so easy for a European to learn to walk barefooted without discomfort, but I acquire tolerance. Then I start to carry things on my head. I take out a pocket handkerchief, fold it into a diminutive pillow and use it as a cushion on which to balance one, two or three books which I place on top of the skull. I then start walking, or sitting down, without upsetting the books. I learn to walk uphill too, and spend my time sensing out the feel of balancing the head with the need to leave the head 'up' and free from volitional interference. This is how fashion models are trained.

In my imagination, I am trying to identify with the physical sensations of 'my Africans' as they walk, sit down, get up and carry. It is an 'African' identification limited to my experience of the Cameroons. But my models could equally well be those beautiful slender Indian women who walk miles with petrol cans of water on their heads and sit down quite naturally in the graceful way that we are trying to re-learn through the Alexander experience. Carrying things on the head seems at one time to have been practised by many races all over the world. Many still retain this form of behaviour. In those continents where people have traditionally always carried things on their heads, we can see that the practice is fast disappearing. So much so that we must be quick to catch the last glimpses of this aspect of man's postural history before mechanisation stamps its mark on us all.

The subject may be examined by looking at the way that burden-carrying of all kinds is performed. Some peoples carry on their heads, some on their shoulders, some in their hands, some on their backs. Finally, there are the Eskimos and Lapps, who move their goods by traction at ground level on the snow and ice. As a wide generalisation, it appears that the points where loads are disposed about the upright human frame are related in some way to the angle of the sun. In the tropics, where the sun is most directly overhead, a large proportion of packages are carried on the head. Moving north, away from the Equatorial belt, one begins to see people carrying lower down the body - for example, water pitchers on the shoulders as one sees in the Mediterranean, North Africa and among Near Eastern peoples. People carrying their shopping baskets in Europe or North America use their lower arms or hands.

These are wide generalisations admittedly, but the urbanisation of towns and the accompanying incursion of traffic have introduced a new element for the first time in human history, affecting the freedom of people to carry things in their traditional ways. Where there is a constant bustle of vehicles, or the rapid movement of crowds, there is no longer a possibility of moving freely with a package or load on the head. I would argue that apprehension of being run over by a vehicle or the fear of colliding with other pedestrians has removed the instinctive freedom of people to carry their packages balanced on their heads. In Britain, the practice died out a long time ago. It is increasingly rare to see a British bricklayer climbing a ladder with a hod-full of bricks on his head, or porters in vegetable and fruit markets balancing their huge baskets of produce. The fashion of carrying large earthenware vessels on the head, as 19th-century people used to do when they brought water from wells, is now totally obsolete. All that remain are a few pictures, such as the scenes painted by Hogarth, to remind us how prevalent it once used to be.

I must confess I still do not understand how or why peoples all over the world ever started to carry things on their heads, but they must do it because it is agreeable to them. The best example I personally encountered in the Cameroons, where this is a stand-ard way of carrying things, was on the gold mine at Betare-Oya. The mine owner had bought some metal wheelbarrows with the intention of improving the hourly production rate of earth moved from the river bed to the washery. Confronted with the novelty of wheelbarrows, which they were seeing for the first time in their lives, the labourers filled them up. But rather than wheel them they put the loaded barrow on their heads and walked the 50 or so metres, where they took them off again and emptied them into the washers. They did not like the 'drag' on their arms and shoulder sockets as they tried to wheel the barrows. Of course, in the name of higher production, they were made to use wheelbarrows in the usual way, but some of them preferred to abandon their jobs rather than adapt to this unfamiliar, tiring method so opposed to their traditional ways. I must say that, in later years, I have come greatly to sympathise with their attitude and to feel that they were probably right to refuse to carry out work which was distressing physically to them.

Clearly, the human frame is being asked to do too much to carry a 50kg or 100kg load on the head for any length of time. Yet, day in and day out, male Africans keep busy at stacking huge heaps of bagged produce and maintain a steady rhythmic stream of work all day. They often chant happily in unison as teams of men carry out head-portering tasks which would be quite beyond the capabilities of Europeans. There is something in the practice of head portering which confers resilience and poise on the individual, be they anAfrican or Indian labourer or a trainee girl mannequin.

Indeed, one of the happiest sights I recall from my travels was in a remote area of southern Morocco, where head portering, as in Europe, has almost died out. On a lonely road, far from a village, a tall young woman walked past me with a load of clothes on her head. Her feline grace was truly remarkable and, while I watched her arms and wrists moving rhythmically as she walked in a state of utter relaxation, I felt that I had come face to face with that true beauty which lies hide behind uninhibited natural motion. I'll never forget the grace of that woman's walk.

All this relates in only a minor way to the discoveries of Alexander. As he gave lessons to his pupils, he made small compressions in the skull by slight downward pressure with his hands. But he was in touch with the same phenomenon which head portering seems to use.

Pygmies do not yet appear to have got round to head portering. One of the leading authorities on pygmies is H.V. Vallois, an anthropologist of international fame who has worked on negrillos and pygmies in the Cameroons. I read up everything he has written. Although the people he has studied principally are the Badjoue, he admits that they are not typically pygmy, either facially or in height or in bodily characteristics. Vallois reports the opinion that the Badjoue have been placed as immigrants from the pygmy areas of the South East Cameroon. But they have resemblances which are studied by Vallois. Once again, I am struck by the realisation that many anthropologists who have written about pygmies have not had the experience of seeing them or the luck to encounter them in their most primitive forms. However, I am fortunate in that I learn that Professor Vallois is soon coming to London to receive the highest honour that the Royal Anthropological Institute can bestow - the Darwin Memorial Gold Medal.

On a dark winter evening, I go by invitation to the presentation ceremony, which is held in the French Embassy in London. After the welcoming pleasantries in English, which Vallois does not seem to understand too well, he reads his paper - in French. Many of the audience will have insufficient command of the French language to follow him closely. But he speaks on the wider aspects of anthropology, as one would expect from an eminent figure, and he does not even mention pygmies. He and I have both been to Nanga Eboko, a one-time recognised locale for pygmy tribes. But after the meeting I cannot summon up the courage to go and congratulate him as he mingles with the guests. I leave the building recognising that I am thinking in a totally different idiom when I juggle with relating the Alexander experience of bringing about postural change to the changes going on in pygmies in Central Africa. It is too 'way-out' as a subject, too lacking in academic structure, to be comprehensible or acceptable to orthodox anthropologists. My other problem is that my ideas are not of interest to teachers of the Alexander Technique either. They would not wish to have seemingly eccentric ideas involved in the work of spreading the technique worldwide. I decide that there is only one thing for me to do - go back to the Cameroons and carry on my own investigation with no outside help and at my own expense. There are no funds to be obtained for crackpot amateur anthropologists.

Out of the blue, quite unexpectedly, comes an invitation from Jean to attend a mineral conference in the Cameroons. He is still in the *Cie Camerounaise Des Minerais* and the Governor has decided to hold a symposium for the benefit of local producers, geologists, officials of the mining bodies in Paris, mining company executives and anyone else with an interest in developing research into mineral resources. I decide to go.

CHAPTER 23

It is now 10 years since I sailed from Africa on that fateful voyage in the Silver Laurel. I look forward to going back with great enthusiasm, for not only shall I have a chance to meet up with old friends, but I shall combine the opportunities of the mineral conference with a trip to the pygmy areas.

Planning a trip by air, via Paris, is the simplest part of the project, although the flight will be long and exhausting in the propeller-driven aircraft. I have a medical check-up, including an X-ray of the chest, and proceed to get vaccinated against smallpox and receive innoculation against yellow fever. It is many years since I underwent either, but the regulations permit me no alternative, even though there never has been any smallpox in the Cameroons.

During these recent years I have been very fit and well, delighting in my marriage and my baby daughter. Business has been thriving and we have bought a new house - very modern and agreeable, with a decent garden to tend and the advantage of giving rapid access to both Victoria and the countryside. My wife has a live-in maid to help with domestic work.

My co-directors view my project to revisit West Africa with some misgivings. I am proposing to leave the business at a time when we are very busy, although only for a month. But they allow themselves to be persuaded that being the only Englishman invited to a French Government conference is rather a distinction. Moreover, we all live with the hope that actuates men involved in mining ventures - that one will 'strike lucky'.

The long, fatiguing Air France flight from London to Douala is made worthwhile by Jean's greeting at Douala airport. He has laid everything on for me and we go to the hotel once owned by his father-in-law to discuss details. Douala is appallingly hot and humid and I begin to feel slightly unwell. I put it down to the fatigue of the flight and after a couple of day's rest I am ready to go to the conference.

It all sounds exciting. The venue is a tin mine in Mayo-Darle, a small property with a well-run flotation plant tucked away in the remote north of the country. The Governor has kindly placed his Heron aircraft at our disposal, and Jean and I with one or two others board the plane for the warm and slightly bumpy journey across one of the least-known parts of Africa.

The conference itself is a minor failure. Not only are there murmurs of drastic political change impending, so that small producers feel insecure about their future, but it soon emerges that there has been no major discovery in the country of the kind of metalliferous mineral wealth which would encourage French or foreign developers to exploit it. It is not felt to be the duty of private firms to undertake basic geological surveys; the Government has officials to do that. Although we are at the tail end of a chain of mineralisation running through Africa, we have to face the fact that the conference has produced no evidence of actual or probable mineral deposits to encourage anyone to put up the money and resources.

I am asked about my earlier venture in the ilmeno-rutile project, and I tell the meeting that I have already caused an investigation to be undertaken by American-controlled capital. Conclusions were that the area was useless. We discuss the possibilities of greater tin resources, but it is plain that our hosts, the Mayo-Darle tin miners, are better placed to look after all the developments which the area has shown as worthy of further investigative work.

By the end of the week, when the conference ends, I am starting to feel quite ill, but having come so far I am not going to give up before I have looked at the rutile prospect on behalf of my company in London. I have planned also to include a trip to the pygmy areas where Vallois worked earlier.

Jean gives me a Landrover and prospecting tackle to take on

my trip. I have my cameras, both still and 8mm movie, and unwell as I feel, I go off on the trip to the Nanga Eboko areas first. Jean cannot come with me. But I have several 'boys' to accompany me, including a driver.

Nanga Eboko is about 150kms from Yaounde. In order to reach the rutile-bearing streams which Jean has prospected, I have to leave the Landrover and walk. I have planned on about seven days walking, but on the first day walk only 12/14 kms. By now, I am starting to feel really ill. I have no idea what is the matter with me, but I have developed a racking cough and am starting to feel totally drained of energy. I continue for two more days, walking at a slow pace and frequently stopping to take a rest. The boys are solicitous and worried about me. They offer to carry me and to make a tipoy out of branches cut from a tree.

By now I am in no fit state to walk far. It is the offer that makes me realise I cannot go on as I am. I have come all the way from England to an abortive mineral conference and have had a struggle to walk to the mineral areas which I now recognise I do not have the strength to reach. I would certainly not have the energy to look for pygmies.

With a desperate feeling of failure and still not comprehending my illness, I let discretion be the better part of valour and turn back to Yaounde. As soon as I have reached the town I pay the boys off and go to bed in the hotel. All the skills at doing Alexander Technique go into these few days and as a result I am able to get to the hospital for a diagnosis.

I tell the doctor at the hospital about my TB and he at once takes X-ray pictures. I am sure I have not got TB as I was checked up just before leaving England. Whilst I wait for the results of the examination, I go to see one or two old friends and acquaintances who, 10 years later, are still living in Yaounde.

Their first exclamations are: "My God, man, you've grown much taller. You look much better in health than you did when you were living here 10 years ago. What a difference living in a European climate has made to you!"

It does not seem appropriate to say how ill I am feeling, but the cough is a giveaway to Jacques, a discerning friend who has experienced TB in his own family.

I am invited to a short drink at the Governor's palace by one of the French administrators, who is anxious to know how the mineral conference has gone. After giving him a brief resumé of my conclusions I tell him that I have been hoping to visit the pygmies, in whom I have taken a much greater interest since I left Africa than during the eight years I lived here. Someone remembers me as the person who used to keep chimpanzees in the garden and I mention that I have been reading and researching into the pygmy status in the phyllum of races. The party ends and the next day I go to the hospital to obtain the results of the tests and X-ray.

"My advice to you," says the doctor in charge, "is to get the first plane home to England. Lose no time. You are very ill. You have positive TB and a large cavitational area in your lungs. You are coughing and you ought to have treatment at once. This climate is death to you if you stay here. Forget about the reasons for which you came here. Go home to England as fast as you can."

Stunned, because only 14 days earlier I left England full of health and vigour, I book a seat home. The Air France hostess is solicitude itself and, since the plane is half-empty, she allows me to lie outstretched on the floor with a blanket over me. How I find the strength to walk across the tarmac at Paris Airport to change into the London-bound aircraft is a mystery? I literally have to shuffle one foot after the other. I am doing all my technique procedures - breathing exercises, directing - remembering all I have been taught by Alexander. I want but one thing - to get into a hospital bed in London, as quickly as possible.

Within hours of arriving at Heathrow I am on my way to hospital and tests soon show that I have indeed succumbed to the old disease. The diagnosis is that the vaccination restored the picture of tubercular lung cavities and stripped the old scar tissue away in a few days. All those patient intense months, even years, of fighting to recover have been torn away by the smallpox vaccination which soon begins to produce other effects as well. A tooth falls out, my eyesight becomes blurred, my brain seems drugged and oppressed and the vaccination scar burns persistently. Confined to bed, I learn that there have been no new developments in England, at least in TB therapy.

My greatest worry is that Alexander died two years before and I feel unable to make the struggle a second time in my life. But I am still only 41.

CHAPTER 24

There is one big difference, however, between the last time I succumbed to this illness and now. The two events are distinguished by the certain knowledge I have gained in the meantime: that the Alexander Technique works. Sensationally for some, miraculously for me.

Sir Thomas and I talk things over. "Why did you not consult me before having a vaccination?" he asks. "It is well known that, for people with a history of TB, vaccination is absolutely contra-indicated." We discuss what is to be done. There are still no effective drugs and, in any case, I am now sick and tired of the medical environment, but I have to recognise that Sir Thomas is kindness itself. With his quiet courtesy, one feels that here is a man who is open and cares.

Once more, I decide to discharge myself from a hospital. After reviewing the state of play with Walter Carrington, who has now taken on the mantle of Alexander, we decide that I had best move into a nursing home near to Walter's private house. He has so much to do in the day, and for me travel to the Alexander Centre is out of the question. So I move into a small private establishment in Ealing, where Walter comes three times a week in the evenings to give me Alexander lessons.

Wonderful, patient, supportive, intelligent Walter, sharing his insights, thinking with me. We take little risks together, using novel ways to go about things. Some elements of courage are often needed; some willingness to try the unknown, for we are stepping all the time into unfamiliar experiences of the body and new unfathomed sensations. How can it be otherwise when one is "directing the brain" to go forward and up within the skull? That is the way of the evolution of the brain - forward with the frontal lobes, up with the cerebellum. "Don't shorten the neck."

In the quiet of a private room, I am free all day to work at 'directing', 'letting-go' and the other releasing processes of the technique.

And after Walter has made his visit, I gradually grow in confidence about my ability to avoid damaging the brain or nervous system. I concentrate on the inner directing work which brings about the deep breathing in the chest, catlike respiratory contractions of the ribs and the unmistakable sensation of spinal fluid pumping along the spine and bathing the brain. It is the nicest way to health that has been devised. Alexander called it "feeling like pussy" - meaning that purring, stilled, contented state of relaxation that domestic cats exhibit.

At the end of a few months, I am well enough to go home again. There has been a somewhat disturbing development concerning the Royal Anthropological Institute, who have received cables from Reuters' agents asking for comment on views I had expressed on the status of pygmies in the Cameroons. The reports arose from gossip at the Governor's party and I am in no state to become involved in publicity which could only be damaging and controversial. I decide that, in the interests of both the Royal Anthropological Institute and myself, I had better resign as a fellow forthwith. Although there is no pressure for such a step, I know that my ideas and experiences are too 'offbeat' to lead to anything but trouble. I am in no fit state to deal with hostile curiosity or downright ridicule.

Most of the doctors I have met, in hospitals or in general practice, have simply not been interested in the Alexander Technique or in the transformations it has brought about in me. I begin to sympathise with the attitude of F.M. who went through so much in the struggle to obtain recognition of his work: that there is something in medical training which closes the mind. That closure results in opinions which assert there can be no way other than the way of the profession. The vast resources, research programmes and prevailing tradition preclude, almost inevitably, the idea that there is any other valid way to deal with illness. No layman such as F.M. Alexander could have developed a technique outside all medical experience which is, on the evidence, often more appropriate and more effective than many of the cut and drug procedures of orthodox medicine. That is the dismissive attitude of most men engaged in the profession of medicine. And perhaps they are right. There are difficulties in applying Alexander's principles on a broad basis to patients in a hospital ward, for instance. Although the technique arises from the use of facilities which lie within each and every human being, not everyone can gain access to those facilities. Alexander himself refused to entertain the idea that his technique was anything other than a means of re-education of the mind-body. He would not keep case histories, although hundreds of successfully taught people had emerged from severe illness able to resume a normal life. He rather resented the use of his time, particularly in the later years of his life, being taken up by sick persons.

CHAPTER 25

Twelve months, almost to the day, since my relapse I have recovered sufficiently to resume my career in business, and opportunities present themselves both to travel and to improve my own personal fortunes. I have undertaken a market survey in North and South America, including the Caribbean, which demands considerable stamina and resilience. Fortunately, I have developed both sufficiently to be able to undertake a tour which involves visiting 27 cities in 42 days.

Moderate success in the next few years has enabled me to purchase a small farm on the borders of Surrey and Sussex. As time passes my wife and I add to the land by acquisitions, and we improve both the house and buildings. Being able to live in one of the most beautiful parts of England and to work in very attractive surroundings in the heart of Mayfair combine to produce an enviable lifestyle. Prosperity, by dint of hard work and good fortune, slowly but surely comes to us. I keep in touch with both of my mainstream interests - physical anthropology, as it might relate to the work of F.M. Alexander, and minerals. The latter involves me in deciding to start a mill to process minerals for industry and, in about eight years, it grows from very small beginnings to an industrial unit which can process some 20,000 tonnes of ore a year.

Business for me has always held challenges which, despite the sedentary life of a manager-owner in Britain, are a compensation for the loss of the freedoms of Africa. Because I would need a vaccination to return to Central Africa, I know that I will never again be allowed to see the country which holds such intense and highly valued memories. And so I have to be content with seeing as many TV programmes as I can which feature Africa, and especially those fascinating series on wildlife. It is commonplace to say that Africa is full of wonders, and gradually the mysteries of the forest and savannah are being revealed. But there are few programmes dealing with pygmies; nor are there any discussions that I can find about their evolution. It is as though there is a blanket thrown over the question of pygmy origins, pygmy development, and the place of the pygmy in human philogeny.

At the beginning of our century, there were still oases of pygmy folk scattered over the world; not just the large concentrations still to be found in the Congo and Cameroon forest areas, but also others in Sudan, Kenya, India and Malaysia. Not all easily conformed to the term pygmy, but small and primitive they undoubtedly were. Such oases have by now dried up, so that there are virtually no pygmies to be found outside the Central African areas of Congo and Cameroon. Whether they have disappeared through failure to adapt or by miscegenation with other people, or whether they have simply changed physically is a subject requiring further study. To my mind, there is no question that the Central African pygmies have changed and are still changing today at a rapid rate, so that their salient pygmy characteristics are fading away. In effect they are metamorphosing.

Metamorphosis is a discredited element in human evolutionary theory. There is no recognised principle, or series of principles, which could effect the rapid changes on a short time scale as implied by the term 'metamorphosis' - except for the discoveries of Frederick Matthias Alexander. Which raises the question: How might the techniques of Alexander be connected with pygmies, in changes to which pygmies are succumbing or even in pre-pygmy primates?

CHAPTER 26

These problems have absorbed me for a further 30 years, so that I have now grown into an old man of 72, still living actively, still undertaking business travel for my mineral company and still enjoying the social pleasures which usually attend successful executives. All through the welter of activities engendered by the competitive life of business there has run the thread of the Alexander experience, which has permeated my thinking and reading.

Shortly after the events of 1955, about which I have written, Walter and I discussed the possibility of my becoming a teacher, but we agreed that the teaching life was not for me and I stuck to my career in business with the Alexander-cum-anthropological roles added. I travelled widely, and whenever I could - in aeroplanes, trains or hotels and during quiet evenings at home and on the farm - I studied and pondered these subjects. It has taken me all this time to arrive at a viewpoint about a possible connection between the Alexander Technique and primate evolution, with particular regard to pygmies.

The ensuing pages are an attempt to make sense of the connection between my own real-life experiences and accepted theories of evolutionary anthropology. However, I must make it patently plain that these ideas are purely my own and quite independent of mainstream theory in Alexander Technique. There is no implication that anyone else, especially those professionally connected with the Alexander Technique, have given approval to this thesis.

In discussions surrounding my views on the subject over many years with several people who appear in this story, above all Walter Carrington, I received some encouragement but did little about it. King-Moir, the Harley Street X-ray man, said: "Write about it." Even Sir Thomas encouraged me, but I did nothing except record events. Walter similarly said: "Write what happened, but recognise that, no matter what you write about theory, you can be sure that no one will read it." So, taking my cue I undertook to make this small contribution to a subject which has fascinated me for a very long time. I have long been mindful of the difficulties surrounding my conclusions. Darwin did not help when he wrote:

> We must not fall into the error of supposing that the early progenitors of the whole simian stock, including man, were identical with, or even closely resembled, any existing ape or monkey. I must point out what is, in fact, self-evident - that not one or all of these still living apes and consequently not one of the so-called manlike apes, can be the progenitor of the human race.

This statement, in the light of what is now known of pygmies and Alexander's work, is a conclusion which may appear to be unduly dismissive. Darwin was of course constrained by the attitude of his Victorian contemporaries. But the present simian stock *has* descended from earlier monkeys and apes, and it is among those earlier stocks that the transformation into man-orientated forms most likely originated. When the transformation occurred, their descendants went on to develop into races of humans. Those who did not transform handed down their unchanged genetic structure to their present representatives - our contemporary stocks of monkeys and apes.

The process of transformation is one which concerns the Alexander student. He is concerned with his own situation, but there is a wider perspective - the transformation process as applied to the original monkey stocks. So it is in one sense correct for Darwin to state that not one or all of the still living apes (or monkeys) can be human progenitors. But that does not remove the possibility that the selfsame simians had ancestors who did make the transformation to become breeding stocks from which our human ancestors arose.

CHAPTER 27

When writing of how he discovered and developed his work, Alexander made no attempt to describe how the 'primary control' works, either in physiological terms, or anatomically. He writes that when he succeeded in preventing the pulling back of his head: "it led to an important discovery which cannot be overestimated. For, through it I was led to discover the 'primary control' of the working of *all* [editor's italics] the mechanisms of the human organism." That is an incredible statement, and for those who have not experienced the technique at the hands of Alexander, it must seem a wildly improbable and unproveable claim. Sight and smell, for example, are just two products of the working of the human organism; but only with difficulty could they be said to be controlled by such a 'primary' mechanism.

However, these considerations do not affect the importance of Alexander's work. They are partly to do with problems associated with terminology. We have to understand the intrinsic importance of Alexander's work itself in terms of the statements it makes, and swallow the verbal bolus of expressions such as 'correct manner of use' and 'primary control'.

Alexander's statements could be summarised as:

1. Correct manner of use is associated with the 'primary control'.
2. The head/neck relationship is central to the working of the 'primary control'.
3. The correct manner of use is attained by inhibition of habitual stimuli and is an essential prelude to initiating change in bodily movement.
4. Inhibition is a mental discipline which, by diligence, can be kept alive in thought, whilst other parts of the brain are engaged in giving 'directions'.

Since such terminology has no place in mainstream technical literature in related areas of research, including that dealing with posture and primatology, we have to find other ways to make a connection between them and the discoveries of F.M. Alexander.

I have written earlier how I personally experienced the 'primary control' in operation. Through it, the tonus of muscles all over the body, from the top of the skull down to the soles of the feet, was changed and I felt the changes as they occurred. It altered the rate of respiration dramatically and enlarged the breathing capacity of the lungs. It changed the pattern of movement of the rib-cage. It aroused the defence mechanisms of the blood, so that infection was overcome. It promoted healing of the damaged tissue. It acted on the ligaments of the spine, straightening it and changing my posture permanently. In sum, it transformed me and restored me to health and vigour from a very critical stage in an incurable illness.

There is a vast chasm between experiencing bodily recuperation as I have described it and making that experience a model for the process undergone by our remote ancestors in their evolution. Nevertheless, whilst recognising that the bodily changes described seem unrelated to the subject of primate evolution, there is in fact an affinity. The anatomical areas involved in arousing the working of the 'primary control' are the same as the areas of the skull and its contents studied in comparative anatomy by primatologists researching primate evolution. For it is on the study of the skull - its muscular attachments, its placing on the top of the spine, the position of the foramen magnum, the growth of the cerebellum, the emergence of the forebrain, the transformation in the shape and size of the brain and a host of related aspects - that the study of primate evolution is centred. It is in that area around the base of the skull, in its muscular attachments and in the shape and size of the brain itself, that the main or 'primary' origins of change are to be located. All other developments of the body and its posture originate in, and derive from, these areas. These are also the areas wherein the 'primary control' is located and whence it exercises its central position of influence over the restoration of the body in the process of applying the AlexanderTechnique.

What, then, could be the process which generates all these influences in two totally different sets of circumstances - the development of the primate brain in evolutionary terms and the recovery from severe illness in a contemporary human body? In my view, the process that is common to both is the circulation of the cerebrospinal fluid from the spinal chord, upward through the brain stem and over the cortex as it bathes the brain on its way to the cisternae. This circulation is initiated by the action of the 'primary control' as the brain stem is lifted, allowing it to penetrate and grow through the floor of the skull. Since the brain stem is the centre which controls respiration, change in its state can initiate changes in the rate and depth of respiration, thereby enabling the thorax to relax. This, in turn, permits deep expansion and contractions of the rib-cage. From this conjuncture of events, the spine can resume its original and essential function. To all intents and purposes one could say that the spine, in addition to its skeletal/structural functions, is a pump. In the evolving primate, it is a mechanism which, metaphorically speaking, sends the sap upwards through the trunk of the spinal chord into the leaves and branches of the brain, located within the skull.

Cerebrospinal fluid, circulating over and through the brain, raises the level of cortical ionisation. It also feeds and nourishes the brain's substance so that it secretes and enlarges. No brain was ever restricted or impeded in its development by its bony skull. The skull has always adapted itself to enlargement of the brain; a fact which was overlooked by earlier anthropologists, who built important but erroneous theories of racial affinities solely on similarities of skull shape.

What evidence, one might reasonably enquire, can be adduced to support such a theory? A possible starting-point might be the thoracic section of the spinal column. One cannot but be struck by the somewhat curious structure between the third and the tenth thoracic vertebrae. The pattern in which the concave facets on the third, fourth and fifth vertebrae give way to the flattened facets on the lower transverse processes on seven, eight, nine and 10, is essentially a mechanical one. The shape and direction of the articular processes limit the degree of motion upwards and backwards or downwards and forwards. Very slight rotation occurs in response to muscle activity attendant upon rib movements in respiration. However, viewed as an engineering plan, the flattened surfaces can have only one functional purpose and that is to push the appropriate vertebrae upwards in the general direction of the head at the precise time that outward breathing occurs. These movements do not measurably happen because of the rigidity of the intervertebral discs and the close-knit ties between the intra-articular ligaments, the longitudinal ligament and the rib heads. However, in young creatures, these joints are more flexible and free and therefore the action of the ribs in respiration imparts an upward thrust on the facets of the lower transverse processes and the vertebral bodies. This is designed for making a mechanical upwards thrust on the spinal column and, by implicated motion, through to the cord. The stimulus to the chord induces cerebrospinal fluid to flow in the direction of the skull. The comparative plasticity of intervertebral joints in young children is matched by a parallel plasticity in some adults. Significantly, this is evident in the peoples of tropical and sub-tropical areas. Extreme examples of this plasticity have been observed in Kalahari bushmen, among whom some females have such plastic inter-vertebral joints that the weight of a heavy meal in the stomach will be sufficient to bend the lumbar region of the spine. The same observation has been made with Central African pygmies.

The plastic quality of the joints of the spinal column is of significance, in that it enables the pumping actions of the ribs, as described above, to make freer and more ample movements. The cerebrospinal fluid can be regularly and plentifully pumped up to the brain. In consequence, the brain, as it is subjected to the gentle flow of a regularly replenished flow of fluid, absorbs the cerebrospinal fluid. In this way the cisternae are supplied and filled, and the brain grows imperceptibly larger as bathing proceeds and fills the skull.

We now have suggested two functions which make changes in the size, shape and structure of the brain. First, the rhythmic wash of the cerebrospinal fluid due to the working of the spinal pump mechanism. Secondly, the 'drawing up' of the medulla into the cranial cavity by the action of the suboccipital muscles working in their anti-gravity function on the cervical spine. If these two conditions are initiated and repeatedly sustained, it would appear that in both human and non-human primates the necessary steps have been taken on the path of evolutionary development, which leads to cranial expansion and postural change. Both cranial expansion and postural change are the key hallmarks of primate evolution and the two are inextricably linked.

We have seen how the Alexander Technique touches upon these two conditions. The 'primary control' is the aspect which sets up the anti-gravity muscle action of the suboccipital muscles and thereby draws up the medulla. This is not at all a dangerous procedure, although the medulla is a delicate and sensitive portion of the brain stem. Impaction in the foramen magnum is usually fatal. However, we are here considering an action which occurs in nature as part of an evolutionary pattern. The slight elongation of the medulla as it moves closer into the cranial cavity induces changes in the rate of respiration: breathing slows and greater volumes of air are admitted to the lungs.

The other 'condition' - the movement of cerebrospinal fluid along the spinal chord and over the brain - is not an unknown phenomenon. Mystics appear to have the capability of inducing a somewhat similar experience in the phenomenon known as arousing the Kundalini. However, for the purposes of this enquiry, we are concerned to examine whether or not there is any connection between the behaviour of non-human primates and the responses of humans who experience the disciplines of the Alexander Technique.

Whilst it is easy to observe the methods of the Alexander Technique at any of the teaching centres, it is not so simple to observe monkeys or apes in order to make evaluative comparisons in this respect. The key task is to observe how humans and non-human primates compare when rising from a sitting position to a standing position, since the essential secrets of the Alexander Technique are buried within that seemingly insignificant movement.

Any pupil going to an Alexander centre is taught that, when rising from sitting to standing upright, the head must not be pulled back. In several sports such as golf or cricket, players are taught not to 'lift the head'. It is surprisingly difficult at first to resist the temptation to avoid doing this, and most people do so however sincerely they wish to avoid it. The whole issue of physical co-ordination is, in fact, a by-product of the relative position of the head as it sits on the neck.

CHAPTER 28

The application of the Alexander Technique to getting up and sitting down leads on to a consideration of how some contemporary primates behave. Many monkeys are more or less capable of some uprightness. In the process of adapting from a life spent largely in the treetops to spending some time on or near the ground, many too have developed their technique for rising from a sitting to an upright position. Some have learned to stand upright in so doing. Most, to be sure, do so in a rather clumsy way compared with humans and, interestingly, the great apes appear to be among the clumsiest. Chimpanzees, although the best of the apes at bi-pedalism, notably contravene the principles outlined by the Alexander Technique. As they stand up or walk for a few paces, they pull their heads back. They also push themselves up from the legs. I tried in Africa to get my own chimpanzees to walk more than a dozen or two yards. We went for a stroll together round the compound every evening, but they soon dropped down into their knuckle four-limbed walking posture. The older they become, the worse they are at standing upright. Monkeys too, although doubtless much better than they were in times such as the Upper Eocene period, when they were treetop dwellers, still retain their salient monkey style of behaviour if they attempt to stand upright or to walk bi-pedally.

Among contemporary primates, we could compile a list of monkey types based on the principle that they both occupy a very diverse range of habitats and have major differences of species between them.

My hypothetical model is based on the view that somewhere within the monkey kingdom lies the latent potential for transformation, in that long ago there were clumps of monkeys who made a transformation, and took their gene pool with them into their new condition. Accordingly, we must consider the possibility that, thereby, they become an ancestor of the world's major races. But if the pygmies of the 19th and 20th centuries were relative new-comers among *Homo Sapiens*, as I believe, then their predecessors must have made the change into pygmy forms in comparatively recent times. The most appropriate species in my view are:

capucin	Central and S. America
mangabeys	E. and W. Africa, Congo
patas	Sub-Saharan Africa
gibbon *(hyloblates lar)*	S.E. Asia
woolly monkey *(lago thrix)*	S. America
lemurs/sifaka	Madagascar
macaques/rhesus etc	Africa, Asia, India
proboscis *(nasalis)*	Borneo, Sumatra
baboons *(papio)*	Africa
langurs *(presbytis entellie)*	India
tamarins *(sanguinas)*	Panama-Columbia
gelada	Ethiopia
guenons *(cercopithecus)*	Africa

In the forests of Malaysia, where monkeys such as long-tailed macaques abound, they are still contiguous with the vestiges of former pygmy populations. In Africa, there is a host of monkey stock with the potential for transformation, living in forest areas adjacent to pygmy peoples. Some monkeys may have performed the transformation miracle by undergoing postural changes equivalent to the technique rediscovered by Alexander. The technique transforms: is it not possible that monkeys have also been subject to its effect?

Those who have followed the argument so far - reinforced by my own direct observations in the Cameroons - may sympathise with a view that modern pygmies, as observed during this century, consti-tute new races of men. They do not need to originate from any ante-cedent hominid or to have descended from prehistoric creatures who were once located in various parts of Africa and Asia or Europe. They seem to have sprung up lightly and rapidly and recently in our midst. They have appeared not only in Africa, but also in parts of Asia. It is true that on the map they appear only as tiny spots of population which have almost dried up. Kenya, Sudan and Malaya have all lost their pygmy populations in recent times. They may have grown in size as part of a natural progression. They have certainly intermarried with locals. But they have certainly changed.

In Central Africa, where they are still to be found in significant numbers, it appears otherwise. An examination of historical anthropological records reveals some striking facts. At the beginning of the century explorers and early anthropologists found pygmies with average heights with yellow skins and below one metre in height. It is not possible to find such a combination today. Maybe today, it is already too late to ascertain the rate at which they have changed. That would require an ability to turn the clock back. The old-style limit of pygmy classification by height was 1.50m, but substantial proportions of the pygmy population covering many different groups were well below this. The contemporary population of the Cameroons is generally thought to have arisen from the Bagielli and Babinga, who were the earliest inhabitants and who still inhabit the southern forests. But whence did the Bagielle and Babinga originate, if not with the pygmies? Today it would be very hard to find anyone like these earlier populations of forest pygmies.

Fast changes and an accelerating speed of life have come to affect mankind, in some degree almost universally, during the past century. These meteoric alterations have introduced new living conditions with accompanying new postural conventions, new foods, the appearance of motorised transport, air travel, new inventions in medicine, radio and television, entirely new industries, new scales of building, new social organisations. No sooner does something emerge than it is replaced by something new. During a period of galloping change on an unprecedented scale such as we have experienced this century, there has been the incredible, unsuspected and largely unnoted change in the pygmies. Not so fast for it to be obvious, yet too fast to be consonant with the rate of slow adaptation which we have always accepted as being true of evolutionary change, according to prevailing models. Whereas there used to be long periods of comparative stasis, in today's world almost everyone undergoes and is affected by constant change.

One of the major changes in the way of life affecting many of the inhabitants of Central Africa has occurred in the Cameroons. When I worked in Yaounde, there was not a single African in a major administrative post of responsibility. It is over 40 years since I left, but in that time there has emerged a self-governing, presidential political system, with a cabinet drawn from indigenous sources, tackling the country's political and economic problems with skill and determination. A huge industry has grown up around hydro-electric power; new factories have sprung up making rubber and tyres, pulp and paper products. Oil refineries and fertiliser plants have been constructed. Towns like Douala and Yaounde are unrecognisable. Where Mme Fischer told me how in 1922 she saw a little pygmy hiding behind a palm tree in Akwa, a suburb of Douala, there is now a huge bridge system and multi-lane motor road with traffic light controls. All that, and much more, in a mere 40 years. Such is the speed of change; not just in West Africa, but all over the world.

All we humans have been changed - at a very fast rate. The yellow pygmy of the Central African forest has changed faster and further than any perhaps, when one considers his lifestyle as described by observers at the turn of the century.

When Darwin developed his theory, it was inconceivable that mankind could be evolving rapidly. Today, we have before us the work of F.M. Alexander, who changed people by changing their posture. He did this by teaching people to stand up and sit down in a specialised way. The changes of evolution no longer require millions of years to manifest themselves. The Alexander Technique, in its widest context, may have relevance now in that it shows us how earlier and slower techniques of adaptation and genetic selection might function alongside other methods of species change. The basic doctrine of man's evolution presupposes that not all experiments in attaining upright posture have been failures. Some, it is posited, must have succeeded. However, it is vitally important to take into account a fundamental principle - that it is by changes in function that structures are modified. Indeed, structural modification - muscular-skeletal transformation - is more than likely to be the consequence of *changed function*. The underlying principle centres around the function embodied in Alexander's term, the 'correct manner of use'. This gives rise to the 'primary control', which in turn is the basis from which structural alterations are initiated.

The 'correct manner of use' introduces vital elements for postural change in all primates which I shall endeavour to describe. For example, instead of the lower limbs being a fulcrum for use as the body rises towards the standing position, the point of lift must be located in and operate from the suboccipital muscles at the base of the skull. Lift-off is achieved by letting the head go forward and up. The antigravity muscles will then lift the body without volitional assistance from pushing up from the legs. Monkeys, generally speaking, will rise from a sitting position to more or less upright position in accordance with their own characteristic patterns of behaviour. This does not exclude, however, the possibility of them achieving postural change through altered function - changing their 'manner of use'. Some seemingly must have done so, although most monkeys, like most humans, use their legs to rise up. The great apes, however, are in a worse case than humans since they grow strong bony ridges on their occipital bones to which the muscles which should serve an antigravity function are attached. In apes, these muscles have a powerful tendency to pull down the skull. Consequently, the great apes have no 'lightness' allowing the skull to 'lift' as posture passes from sitting to upright positions. Unless, and until, the uninhibited release of the suboccipital muscles has been learned as a skill, the other elements for transformation cannot be put in place. This is true of men, monkeys and apes. The 'primary control' cannot operate from the legs, and observation of primates shows that they move from sitting to standing by the aid of thrust in the legs. As Alexander might have said: They 'do' from the legs rather than 'let' from the head.

If we can set aside for a moment the hypothetical model contained in orthodox evolutionary theory and look towards monkeys, both past and present, as the possible source of all human races, we have a quite new scenario. It does not invalidate the orthodox scenarios, but it inserts a different dimension to the problem. What is being suggested here is that man has evolved separately in the main continents in which he still finds himself. He has done this at different times and in several different places. He has also done so from different monkey stocks. This alternative and vital process is embodied in the transformation of certain species of monkey. The point is that we may have bypassed the ape. The concept being proposed is that the different races of mankind each have their origin in distinct and separate species of monkey. As we have seen, the potential stock in the pool of monkey species was long distributed throughout much of the world. The pool has been available for millions of years.

There is still the question of the hominids, whose remains have been located in many areas of the world. Like pygmies, numbers of hominid types seem to have flourished for a while and then perished. If the step from monkey to hominid is to be considered, we might ask ourselves what light can be cast on a possible hominid/pygmy relationship.

If new races of pygmy have appeared in recent times, our only clue to the pre-pygmy stage is in the scant reports from Africa which have been discussed in Chapter 21. May it not be, however, that modern life has by now learned to bypass the hominid stage and go from monkey to pre-primitive pygmy in a single leap? Such a development would be consonant with many of the telescopic effects which life has introduced in some of its other manifestations. In modern times, the pre-primitive pygmies may be the evolutionary alternative to hominids. They may not have the need to spend vast periods of time in order to progress; they may have been able to take advantage of the time spent by some hominids to make the monkey/primitive pygmy change efficiently and rapidly. As was said earlier, life learns its lessons.

It is not necessary to postulate migrations of early hominids or early Man starting from 'early dawns' in East Africa and radiating through the world. Our origins as humans in clumps of races can all be traced to our origins in clumps of monkeys. Whilst we are all racially distinct from each other in origin, what is common to each race in each continent is the process of transformation in our evolution. And it is this process which confers on us our common humanity.

If we start with monkey stocks *in situ*, we have to consider ways in which they could have been transformed to give rise to pre-primitive man. If we believe that the discoveries of F.M. Alexander have relevance, we can at least see that monkeys do not have what he would describe in humans as 'bad habits' of 'manner of use' to unlearn. They are not so conditioned as to need to transcend these impediments, which we humans learning the Alexander Technique have to master as a prerequisite, through the 'no' saying process. Monkeys have a subtle advantage over men here.

Monkeys changed in response to the exigencies of their environment. The reciprocal of that interchange was the change in the environment itself. The two sides to this environmental equation are: the earth and its prevailing conditions, which have always provided the basic stimulus to life's development at its many levels, and those species of monkey that have given rise to the sort of pre-primitive 'upness' that one gets after a lesson.

Slowed-down film exposures have shown the types of movement which vervets and macaques fuscata display. Both use their legs to stand up - not their heads. They both pull their heads back when they rise. Because their postural behaviour contravenes this Alexander precept, they fail to make changes. In choosing macaques and vervets, we are selecting but two out of the 51 genera of living primates. Doubtless others of the contemporary primates contain members who could have served as a model, as well or better. They were chosen because not only are they both capable of bi-pedalism, but there is pictorial and film evidence which can be used to study them in detail.

Monkeys who live mainly in trees cannot enjoy the conditions for postural development, even if they come down occasionally to ground level. Monkeys, whether past or present, living largely as tree-dwellers are not immediately of interest. To live in a tree, balanced on a branch, is to have a precarious foothold compared with a plantigrade posture. Using feet to secure a firm purchase on a branch changes the stance, and eliminates the possibility of using the head as the starting-point of passing from sitting to standing. Monkeys, even those who dwell in savannah or adopt the 'leaping' characteristic, have a long way to go before they can learn to walk upright other than by using their hind legs to propel themselves. The sifaka of Madagascar, a member of the indriidae and a prosimian, is a vertical leaper and clinger that also stands upright. In slow motion film, the sifaka has an arresting mode of progression, but it still uses its powerful hind legs to stand up.

For millions of years, the vervets, the macaques, and the sifakas have inhabited those special areas of forest and woodland or savannah where flat ground for bi-pedal learning was available. Both monkeys have had their predators, but in the time they have been on the earth there must have been locations and periods when they were safe from punishing levels of predation. Part of the atmosphere for evolving a head 'going up' behaviour relies on quiet, on 'feeling safe', and on warmth.

CHAPTER 29

East Africa saw the discovery in 1925 of the Taungs skull by Raymond Dart, himself a pupil of F.M. Alexander and a staunch supporter of the Alexander Technique. At the time, the skull was very significant, being considered an infant man-ape and the first to be found in Southern Africa. Subsequently, discoveries by the industrious Leakey family, Robert Broom and others were given various dates for their origins. Some dated from between one and three million years ago, with the Taungs skull less than one million years old. Later, more relics were found and the range of Australopithecines - Erectus, Robustus, Boisei, Afarensis, to name some of the pre-eminently significant - were from African locales.

The next finds were made in Asia, first in the 1920s by Davidson Black and again in 1929 when Pei Wen-Chung identified a further ancient skullcap. The Peking skeletons have been given the name of Sinanthropus Pekinsis, 'hominids' with 'erect postures' and have been dated from 200,000 to 500,000 years ago. Hominids found in China were given much more recent origins than those in Africa, a fact which gave rise to theories of migration whereby the latter migrated in the interval to form populations in various areas round the world, including Asia. If we set aside the notion of migration on so extraordinary a scale and replace it with the concept of monkey transformation from stocks which were already present in each of the main locations, we have a more rational explanation of the origin of present and past races of the world. The Alexander Technique confers the potential for transformation, and across the ages various types of monkey would have had time, opportunity and scope to develop the skill of getting up from a sitting posture and doing it from the head. The reverse aspect of sitting down from the head - starting from the upright position - is part of the specialised way of getting the system 'to work'.

This is not the place to discuss the changes in the nervous

system itself - nor to elaborate the participation of altered components of the brain (e.g. the pituitary) as the brain enlarges. The modifications postulated are indeed very great and seemingly impossible when one looks at any of the monkeys as they stare back from behind the bars of their cages in zoos. However, we should not be put off by the presence of bodily fur or tails, since the growth of both is inhibited when the total system makes its transformation.

It is known that large changes are recorded within the human phyllum. Skeletal records bear witness to this. The Alexander Technique, as applied to primate evolution, points to a novel direction in the way and speed of change. Apart from the influences mentioned above, it may well be that other external circumstances have entered into the equation. Whilst it is not within the scope of these notes to postulate interventions from outside the earth's environment, it does seem probable that other elements have brought their energies to bear. For example, it seems unlikely that the solar system has played no part in our evolution other than to provide heat and light. We see extra-terrestrial influences manifesting in the tides and upon gravity, for instance. We know of an abundance of energies raining constantly on to the earth and affecting all life - ultraviolet rays, cosmic particles, infra-red and gamma rays and so on. It is inconceivable that life's evolutionary activity has not been influenced by these other forms of energy, but we do not yet know what part they have played in our development. At all events, the growth of the primate brain, attributable in part to changes wrought by the processes rediscovered by Alexander, can be considered to have grown in preparation for the elaboration we all know has taken place.

POSTSCRIPT

In reviewing what I have written, I am mindful of the fact that I might appear to have treated some of my sources in a cavalier fashion, albeit unintentionally. For that I ask forgiveness. On the subject of the pygmies of Central Africa, many devoted and expert observers have published the results of painstaking work in the field and their conclusions are a long way from mine. Deserving of special mention is Ajoulat, who was a doctor with a special interest in physical anthropology. As he worked for a long time in the Yokadouma area, he had ample opportunity for observing the pygmies of the region. He roundly declared he had never seen any yellow pygmies or heard of them in the Yokadouma area (verbal report). His work on the Babinga and Bagielli, supported by his colleague, Dr. Chabeuf, revealed that men and women did not differ very much in height from the other types measured by Poutrin, Kuhn, Pales, Weber, Vallois and Lalouel. These were all in *Babinga of the Forest,* sampled over a vast area in different parts of the Ituri. Lalouel does, however, make it plain that "our Babinga belong to a race of little men, who are taller than the pygmies of the Ituri." The range in stature was 1.455m (Weber) up to 1.579m (Fleuriot).

But no one has devoted any significant attention to the fact that pygmies in Cameroon and elsewhere have evolved in recent times from smaller figures; that they have rapidly changed colour from yellow to black; that their limb proportions have altered in a few generations; and that their environment has undergone enormous transformations. These are all clearly of great significance.

Similarily, in elaborating the Alexander Technique I have said nothing about the phenomonon in which, almost as a by-product, energies are transmitted to and through the hands of the teacher as he communicates his or her skill.

In the section dealing with my experience of TB, I have perhaps

been unduly dismissive at times of medical achievements, but have been grateful enough for their intervention. In particular, I should mention the anti-TB drugs which were developed in the 1960s.

If I were asked to choose the cause on which I would prefer to focus attention, it would not be physical anthropology, for the simple reason that I could hardly expect any response other than the issue of warnings against the dreadful consequences of unproven generalisations.

Nor would I choose the cause of the Alexander Technique, as it is by now so well established in the world that it will progress by its own momentum and does not need my championing.

Nor would I wish to further influence - if such were possible - any part of the orthodox medical profession, which is already under sufficient pressures from complementary medicine. (Although I would dearly like them to find some of my X-ray pictures which they lost).

No, I would hope for a change in attitude towards the destruction of tropical forests and monkey habitats. The continuing capture of primates - said to be approximately 500,000 per annum - for laboratory and other purposes, allied with ecological pressures, means that soon we shall lose most of the monkey populations of the world. Would that some of the respect displayed by Indian religious sects towards the hanuman langur could be extended by the rest of humanity to the world's monkey populations. That would be a truly meaningful gesture with which to show reverence and to recognise our obligations towards both the forces of Life and our indirect forebears.